The
Executive
Guide to
E-MAIL
Correspondence

Including

Model Letters

for Every

Situation

BY

Dawn-Michelle Baude, Ph.D.

CAREER
PRESS

Franklin Lakes, NJ

THE EXECUTIVE GUIDE TO E-MAIL CORRESPONDENCE
EDITED AND TYPESET BY ASTRID DERIDDER
Cover design by Howard Grossman/12E Design
Printed in the U.S.A. by Book-mart Press

To order this title, please call toll-free 1-800-CAREER-1 (NJ and Canada: 201-848-0310) to order using VISA or MasterCard, or for further information on books from Career Press.

CAREER PRESS

The Career Press, Inc., 3 Tice Road, PO Box 687,
Franklin Lakes, NJ 07417
www.careerpress.com

Library of Congress Cataloging-in-Publication Data

Baude, Dawn Michelle, 1959-
    The Executive guide to e-mail correspondence : including model letters for every situation / by Dawn-Michelle Baude.
        p. cm.
    Includes bibliographical references and index.
    ISBN-13: 978-1-56414-910-7
    ISBN-10: 1-56414-910-2
    1. Electronic mail messages. 2. Letter writing. I. Title.

HE7551.B38 2006
651.7'9--dc22   2006023656

Dedication and Acknowledgments

Over the years, I've had the opportunity to coach writers whose e-mail documents were a career liability. Their e-mails were either heavily revised before being sent through the chain of command, or they were bounced back for more and more rewriting. These poor writers were extremely intelligent, highly motivated people who excelled in other aspects of their jobs. Only their writing held them back.

After learning a few e-mail writing techniques and how to apply them, these writers went on to succeed and, in some cases, receive company-wide commendation for their written documents. In other words, workers singled out for poor communication skills became writers praised for the high quality of their e-mail.

I dedicate this book to them.

I owe my gratitude to colleagues, friends, and students who have contributed their advice and insight to this project. Special recognition is extended to the IBM EMEA Legal Team, including Carl Belding, Dan Schenck, Fabio Moretti, Eva Salzmann, and Paloma Valor, for introducing me to the issues that this book addresses.

I would also like to thank the INSEAD and Harvard Alumni Groups, Michael Herlihy at International Chemical Corporation, and Victor Sonsino at the European Counsels Group, for providing ideas and perspective.

My appreciation goes to Dr. George Lakoff, Kathleen Frumkin, and Dr. Kyoko Inoue, for encouraging me to rethink English grammar for myself. I also want to thank Tanis Kmetyk, who is an ongoing source of editing insight and advice.

And finally, I extend my gratitude to Gina Panettieri at Talcott & Notch Literary Agency, and the top-flight crew at Career Press, for their cheerful suggestions, encouragement, and feedback.

Contents

How to Use This Book

Look no further: everything you need to write clear and efficient e-mails is between the covers of this book!

Models *show you how it's done.*

 Maps *provide flexible document outlines for every e-mail task.*

Tools *explains the why and how of e-mail English.*

Netiquette *describes e-mail trends.*

Options *illustrates how to swap words and phrases.*

Inbox *helps control the impression your e-mail makes.*

Edit *shows you how to revise your e-mail.*

Advice *supplies practical guidance on essential writing issues.*

Introduction

E-mail is not hard copy

Don't make the mistake of thinking that an e-mail is just a document you read on a computer screen. Because it's not. E-mail is designed to move or transact information as rapidly as possible from writer to reader. E-mail usually produces immediate action, often in the form of another e-mail.

Hard copy is designed for contemplation over time. Hard copy does not necessarily move the reader to act. Readers don't immediately respond to hard copy with more hard copy, if ever. E-mail is a *transaction*; hard copy is a *reflection*.

E-mail is more than rectangular

E-mail appears in a window, with clearly defined edges. The window is on a screen, and the edges of the screen are reinforced. The edges of the computer conceal armatures that hold the screen in place. These edges and frames—windows and screens—focus reading in a way that is very different from the way we read hard copy. The edge of the piece of paper, of the book or booklet, is not so insistent. It's easier for the eye to lift, to wander, to reflect.

Boxed-in

In e-mail, multiple frames relentlessly focus the eye on the text. Rigid borders confine our gaze, keep it on the words. The trapped-in quality of the text affects our expectations about the purpose and intent of reading. When we look at an e-mail, we expect to receive information—right away. And we get frustrated when we don't get it.

E-mail in the box

The frame pops open; the e-mail appears. In a click, the window closes and it's gone. The ephemeral character of e-mail means it can't waste time. It either rapidly communicates, or it doesn't communicate at all.

E-mail is not quaint

Since e-mail and hard copy don't deliver information in the same way, they're not written in the same way either. Everything from layout to sentence patterns to vocabulary changes. For example: long, ponderous paragraphs don't work well in business e-mail—it's better to divvy the text up into smaller units. And standard hard copy letter formulas, such as "Yours very truly," sound quaint in e-mail. It's better to go with "Regards." In business e-mail, efficiency of communication takes precedence over literary style and social conventions.

Do-it-yourself reading

To communicate information rapidly, let the reader direct his or her own reading. Map the document so that the reader intuitively knows where to look for specific information. Simplicity gives the reader freedom to navigate the e-mail without wasting time.

To skim and scan

Skimming means that the reader gives different levels of attention to different parts of an e-mail. Some sentences receive a close, word-by-word, focus—other sentences aren't read at all. Scanning means the reader is looking for specific information and ignoring the rest. For example, a reader may skim an itinerary in an e-mail from a travel agent and scan for the price of airfare. Knowing how to set-up a business e-mail for skimming and scanning is a highly sought after skill.

More white space, please

In order to skim and scan, the eyes need to be able to move around the text. The eyes want to focus in some places, rest in others.

A dense block of print on the screen does not encourage rapid eye movement. It's impossible to jump around, because there's nowhere to jump to. The reader has no choice but to continue, sentence by sentence, word by word. It plods. It takes time.

Contrast speeds things up. Alternating print with empty white space gives the reader wings. In the rhythm of black text and white space, attention can vary with curiosity. The eye has freedom to alight here and there in the text, instead of just dutifully soldiering on.

White space is meaningful

White space is not empty. It's full of meaning. White space tells the reader that there's a change in idea, a shift in the argument, an example on the way, a contrast coming, or an objection being raised. Readers use white space to navigate information in an e-mail as much as they use printed words on the screen.

First things first

Years of reading practice have taught us to emphasize first-things in a text. In business e-mail, the first sentence of the text is more important than the fourth sentence in the third paragraph. And the first sentence in any paragraph is usually more important than any other sentence in the same paragraph.

Readers skim first sentences in paragraphs to decide if they need to take more time to read the paragraph slowly in its entirety. And readers will also decide to read an e-mail immediately or save it for later based on the first sentence.

The paragraph rule

The business e-mail paragraph often moves from a general idea to specific ideas, or from the most important idea to least important. The most general or important sentence goes first. The other sentences amplify the idea, extend the idea, compare or contrast the idea, or support the idea.

Of course, not every single e-mail paragraph follows the general-to-specific, or most-to-least important pattern. But that doesn't mean the reader doesn't pay attention to the first sentence of each paragraph anyway. In fact, it's very hard not to. Ever since we learned to read, we've been taught to pay close attention to the first sentence. And we do!

Readers are creatures of habit

Want a reader to notice a particular point? Put it at the top of the e-mail or in the first sentence of a paragraph. Want to hide a point you still have to make? Bury it in the fourth sentence of the third paragraph.

Announce your subject

The most important sentence in an e-mail is the first one. It often decides whether your reader will read on grudgingly or with interest. In fact, it decides if your reader will read on at all! For that reason, the first sentence announces the main point of the e-mail. Readers want to cut right to the chase. Occasionally, the subject announcement may extend to two sentences, but one sentence is preferable.

Make sure the intent is clear

Begin with your conclusion, then explain.

—For replies, give your answer in the first sentence and explain your reasoning below.

—For requests, telling the reader straight out what you want saves everyone time.

—For updates, summarize the situation in the first sentence and then detail it in the rest of the e-mail.

—If you have a question to ask, do so right away.

—If the reader has asked you to reply, remind him or her at the start.

Attention diminishes with length

The longer you carry on, the less likely the reader is paying attention.

Headers can help

Using headers—or subtitles—enhances skimming. Headers give readers clues about e-mail content so that they can make decisions about what they want to read, the order in which to read, and the material they don't need to bother with.

For example, you could label paragraphs with headers describing stages in a process, such as "Problem," "Analysis," and "Solution." Or you could use paired headers, such as "Assets" and "Liabilities," or even "Action" and "Outcome." Dates, or steps in a sequence, also work well.

E-mail's odd relationship with print

Business e-mail has, in fact, spawned its own writing conventions, such as signature lines with the information that once appeared at the top of hard copy, such as snail-mail addresses and phone numbers. Semicolons, already on the wane in hard copy correspondence, are rare in e-mail, while the dash is rapidly gaining ground. As generations who have never known a world without the Internet hit the marketplace, they'll continue to shape language to our evolving digital needs.

A little less formal

E-mail is more like sticking your head through a colleague's office door than introducing yourself at a conference table. It remains polite and dignified, but it often loses many of the trappings of hard copy correspondence. One-word sentences or paragraphs, for example, are okay. Roman numerals (I. II. III.) look fussy in e-mail, while Arabic numbers (1. 2. 3.) work just fine. Or, better yet, drop the numeric system altogether and go with a simple bullet point (•).

Simplify, simplify, simplify

An excellent test of a writer's skills is the ability to translate complex subjects into straightforward prose. In business e-mail, the smartest writers use short sentences and common vocabulary whenever possible.

Short = fast

Short sentences keep ideas on track—for the writer as much as for the reader. They're a quick remedy against grammatical issues clogging long, convoluted sentence structures. Short sentences don't usually have as many grammar issues, if any at all. They speed along, unencumbered by pretentious—or misguided—mass.

Length matters!

Because e-mail is designed to be skimmed, screen-size document length is preferred. Long e-mails should be divided up into short, concise e-mails whenever possible. Supporting information, the backstory, and contextual documents should be relegated to attachments—they stay off the center stage (or in this case, out of the active window). A short e-mail targets its subject, allowing the reader to hit the reply button right away. No scrolling necessary.

Hold the fancy vocabulary

"Perspicacious" is a great word, but "sharp" is better in a business e-mail context. The idea isn't to impress the reader with semantic subtlety and texture—the idea is to get the message across, right away. Longer words take more time to process than short words. We don't have to spend a sliver of neural time to observe, "Wow—haven't seen that word in a while!" We just keep right on going.

Keep the tense simple

The trend toward simplicity in e-mail English extends to verb tense. Who needs "He would have been phoning" when "He phoned" will do? Simple present and past tenses can do a lot of the tense work in English. They're shorter, quicker, and less apt to fall victim to grammatical error. Their authority shines through.

What's with indents?

The indent at the beginning of the hard copy paragraph has gone the way of envelope. It's a relic of how we used to communicate in the past, not the way we'll communicate in the future...at least as far as e-mail is concerned. Why? Because the eye needs a full empty line between paragraphs to skim.

Dear Reader

The elaborate salutations of hard copy correspondence are disappearing. For example, instead of "Dear Mrs. Notley," or even "Dear Alma," in a business e-mail, just "Alma" will do, even when the correspondents don't know each other personally. Most business e-mail favors a comma after the name, unless the writer is trying to send a signal of high formality— then the colon comes into play. "Alma:" tells the reader that something very important is about to follow, while "Alma," signals business-as-usual.

More e-mail, fewer windows

Because one e-mail leads to another e-mail, back-and-forth e-mail is common. In an e-mail thread, a record of the previous installment is pasted in below the most recent e-mail. That way, you can trace the development of ideas without having to click open each e-mail individually.

More e-mail, less formality

As the e-mail thread lengthens, a curious thing happens—the e-mail installments tend to shrink. New installments in a thread don't function as new e-mails. They operate as extensions of the original mail.

First to go are the names. Sometimes the writer will use initials, but often markers of identity disappear altogether from the active frame. Sentences simplify, reduce. Markers of context, such dates and times, are often omitted. There's no need to identify or reinforce the parameters of the initial e-mail over and over again. If the readers lose the thread, they can check the previous e-mails.

Intertextual and hypertextual

An e-mail usually doesn't exist in literal isolation, as hard copy does. It is explicitly *intertextual*, in the sense that it links to previous e-mail in the same window. It is explicitly *hypertextual*, in the sense that it's apt to include attachments or links to Websites. Because e-mail is both intertextual and hypertextual, content often does not have to be continually reiterated, because the reader already has access to all the information in the current window.

Cut the thread

Long e-mail threads take on historic value. But they can quickly become heavy. There's a point at which the back-and-forth of correspondence has only a residual value. No one is going to scroll through it all, even when the issue is of primary concern. To avoid dragging a useless tail around, cut the e-mail thread now and then. Begin a fresh, new e-mail. That way, when readers need to sift through the sand, they'll be more likely to find the true value.

What about the subject field?

Subject fields in e-mail function like titles in hard copy. Most often, the subject field summarizes the topic of the e-mail ("May 14 Committee Meeting"). It can also pique the reader's curiosity by asking a question ("Lumina Going Public?"), comment on an aspect of the content ("Yesterday's Security Breach"), quote directly from the content ("5-Step Background Checklist"), or demand the reader's attention by announcing urgency ("Urgent M&A Update").

Sometimes writers want to draw attention to the personal nature of their mail. In this case, they often use their names ("From Pres. Wilkins"); titles ("From the VPs Office"); or coded, personalized references ("About

Our Project"). Other times, the readers don't bother to type in a subject field, so the computer does it for them, "Re: From the VPs Office."

The problem with subject lines

The busy reader doesn't always read them.

Playing the style game

Vocabulary, sentences, punctuation, and layout can all be modulated for style. The closer the conventions are to hard copy, the more formal the e-mail. Add a semicolon, and it veers toward formality. Sign your e-mail with initials, and you've opted for informality. Use italics instead of capital letters for emphasis, and you look very formal. Put in a lot of dashes and you're informal. Having a feel for the signals words, sentence structure, punctuation, and layout give allows you to have more control over the impression your e-mail makes.

Errors in email?

The speed with which e-mail is written, sent, and read seems to invite error. Even the most scrupulous writers can press the send button before they correct the grammatical error in the fourth sentence. The grammar check missed it, too. Occasional errors, while undesirable, are not uncommon. Continual errors, however, are worrisome and suggest the writer needs serious writing help.

Can you see what you're writing?

The quickest way to find errors in your e-mail is to consult the copy of the e-mail you've already sent. Once the pressure is off to send, you see the e-mail baldly, for what it's worth, in all its shame and glory.

When we're trying to bang out an e-mail to send, a different situation inheres. We type too fast. We read too fast. We proof too fast. Our dyslexia, corrective lenses, eye strain, overindulgence from the night before, and lack of sleep get the better of us. Oh no! It's too late. Not even the grammar and spellchecks can save us. It's gone.

Perhaps one day our e-mail programs will psychological delays tagged to the stress or sleepiness of the writer. Until then, we have to help ourselves by:

—changing the typeface of the e-mail to see the contents afresh when we edit and revise

—changing the type size for the same reason

—printing out a hard copy

—reading the e-mail aloud so that the ear can hear errors that the eye can't see

Put out the fire

Flaming is a no-no. No matter how angry, insulted, and indignant you are at the e-mail you just received, fight the temptation to let off steam. Mean and angry e-mails are easily dismissed—it's the cool, calm ones that get revenge. And sometimes, a pleasant, understanding e-mail catches your adversary off guard. The last thing you need at work is a reputation as a flamer. Coworkers will sift through the ashes and gossip.

Frames magnify

Emotion comes across in e-mail with more force than we often imagine. It's almost as if the focused reading produced by framing in screens and windows intensifies emotion rather than diminishes it. What may have seemed like an aloof observation could strike the reader as downright rude. The off-hand complaint could come across as aggressive. A little bit of emotion goes a long way in business e-mail.

When to pick up the phone

—When you need to communicate how you feel.

—When you need to break bad news before you send the e-mail.

—When you've been e-mailing someone back and forth for weeks.

What's left in an e-mail once all the nonessential words have been taken away?

A clear message.

A startling observation

A lot of the business e-mail circulating right this second through cyberspace can be halved in length. Some business e-mail can even be reduced even further, provided the writer knows what to look for.

If business e-mails were more concise, there'd be less e-mail stuffing the inbox. All the time wasted with replying, with correcting miscommunications, with complementing incomplete communications, and/or dithering in order to delay the Herculean task of communication could be invested in other activities.

E-mail is economic

The economy is based on transactions of goods and service. You want to get the most for your money. You want to spend as little as possible and maximize the returns. The same thing is true in e-mail. You want to get maximum returns on the fewest words possible. That's just good business, and good communication.

CHAPTER ONE

The Basics

INCLUDING

Request for Approval

Reply to a Request for Approval

Request for Information

Reply to a Request for Information

Request for Approval

Subject
Announcement

Bree,

I need your urgent support on an issue regarding a nationwide rebate program. I don't believe we should approve additional rebates for the southern region because of potential business partner issues.

Background

A nationwide 1% rebate program is scheduled to launch in February 2008. Because of storm damage, the time frame in the southern states has been extended. An additional 0.5% rebate is to be offered in March and April in the southern region.

Problem

Due to slack markets in disaster areas, the southern states want a 1.5% rebate *throughout* the duration of the program. Business, including Sikibu, is behind it. In response to the pressure, Promotions and Discounts has come up with a "region- and state-only promotions policy."

Analysis

The extended 1.5% rebate for the southern region doesn't meet the region-specific promotions criteria—various functions are fighting against it. Our business partners will not understand preferential treatment given to the southern region. BP problems may impact the AWP deal.

Goodwill
Close

The attached notes provide full details and discussion. Please let me know if you need additional information.

Regards,

Max Jacovitch
Director, LAT Unit
Vector, Inc.
maxjacovitch@vector.com

Tools

Immediately announce that you want approval for a particular course of action

Stating at the get-go what you want and why you want it gives the boss an important option: He or she can reply without reading the rest of your e-mail. What? The boss reply without reading the reasons behind your request? After you've taken all that time to figure it out? After you've noted your reasons down in the hopes of dazzling him or her with the brilliance of your analysis?

Yes, of course, the boss might scan your e-mail for specific information, decide to read the entire e-mail thoroughly, or even ask for more information. But most of the time, the boss just wants to know *quickly* what you think. That's why you were hired.

Use headers to map the document

Headers allow readers to zoom in on relevant information. There's no need for the readers to waste time wading through an entire e-mail to find a particular point. Oftentimes, readers don't want to read the entire document. The boss, in particular, is looking for specific information in order to make a decision.

Not every detail is as important as the others. Headers allow the reader to pick and choose the parts of the document that should be skimmed and the parts that need to be considered in detail. They allow readers to direct their own reading of a document, rather than accepting one imposed on them.

How to map a document

If you don't have a model, you have to come up with the map yourself. Mentally reduce your document to its main points and arrange them in a logical order. Identifying the main points is often the hard part. For example, in an e-mail to a colleague recapping a verbal agreement, you begin by dating the meeting in the first paragraph. Then assign one paragraph to each point that you agreed to. Conclude on an upbeat note. Eventually, structuring a document will come so naturally, you won't even have to think about it.

Keep headers short

The simplest kind of header summarizes information that's elaborated in the following paragraph. But be careful—a summary header directs reading, but it doesn't give the content away! If your headers get too long and complex, you're probably writing the lead sentence in a paragraph.

Make sure the headers stand out

A header that blends into the rest of the text isn't functioning as a header. You can put the headers in bold. They can also be underlined, italicized, or capitalized. Headers are usually either anchored on the left-hand margin or centered.

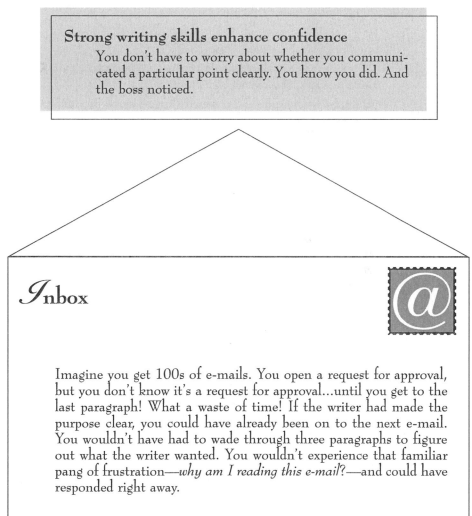

Strong writing skills enhance confidence
You don't have to worry about whether you communicated a particular point clearly. You know you did. And the boss noticed.

*𝓘*nbox

Imagine you get 100s of e-mails. You open a request for approval, but you don't know it's a request for approval...until you get to the last paragraph! What a waste of time! If the writer had made the purpose clear, you could have already been on to the next e-mail. You wouldn't have had to wade through three paragraphs to figure out what the writer wanted. You wouldn't experience that familiar pang of frustration—*why am I reading this e-mail?*—and could have responded right away.

Reply to a Request for Approval

Ray,

Subject Announcement

I accept your recommendation regarding the new Vector total cap.

Reasoning

In general, we never want to pay damages that exceed the purchase price of product/service.

Context

The "per claim" language dates from the time when we sold more products than services. The language is less risky for products, where multiple claims from the same product are rare. This is not the case with services, where multiple claims are likely. In SO, SI and Consulting, we obviously have a different approach because of the nature of the engagement.

Goodwill Close

The total cap is definitely the better way to go. Let me know if you need more.

Regards,

Andrei Seligmann
Negotiation Analyst
Vector, Inc.
andreiseligmann@vector.com

*T*ools

Grant or decline approval right away

Someone who's asked for approval wants to know one thing: *Has approval been granted*? Tell the reader at the get-go!

Reminding the reader specifically what you are agreeing to and why you're agreeing helps avoid any misunderstandings in the future.

Taking a moment to succinctly explain your decision fosters constructive relationships as well as builds the knowledge base.

Keep paragraphs short

Short paragraphs allow for skimming and scanning. Short paragraphs fit better in screens and windows. Even more importantly, the short paragraph suggests that you've taken the time to organize your document into digestible content bytes.

A short paragraph can be as short as one sentence or one word. It can be as long as three or four sentences. If your paragraph is longer than that, see if you can break it into two or more separate, consecutive paragraphs.

Short paragraphs allow reader and writer to distinguish—and literally focus on—key information. Short paragraphs are friendly, thrifty, and neat.

Arrange paragraphs in the order of importance

Look at it this way: Readers who spend a lot of time on the screen pay more attention to the opening of a document than they do to its close. For example, they may read the first sentence in its entirety. But by the time they reach the end of a document, they're probably just catching a few words here and there. All the more reason to prioritize your information according to importance.

The essential point of the e-mail goes at the top. The rest of the information is often arranged in paragraphs according to a descending order of importance. Or as one VP told me, "The first sentence is what counts. The rest is just details."

Humanize technical information by dividing it up

The jargon—or technical vocabulary—of business can put off even an interested, knowing reader. Even when you know what the jargon means, it still has a tendency to repel. And if you're not certain what the jargon means, it can be downright alienating.

One way to avoid deterring the reader is to confine jargon in manageable units. Small units help us feel in control of the information, instead of the other way around.

Even when readers aren't familiar with the jargon, small paragraphs and short sentences make them feel as if they could be.

Options

I accept….	You've got a green light to…
OK…	I'll give you my approval on…
Do it…	I'm alright with that…
I agree…	You have my OK on…
I approve…	Proceed with…
I concur…	Go ahead and…

Caught off guard

Many professionals have been in the hot seat because of e-mail. Common mistakes include:

—withholding the purpose of the e-mail until the conclusion

—writing the e-mail too fast, so the result is sloppy and unclear

—trying so hard to be clear that the message is lost in an avalanche of detail

—lumping the e-mail into one text block instead of dividing it up into paragraphs

—omitting crucial information for fear of making writing mistakes

—putting the right information in the wrong order

—repeating information needlessly or unconsciously

—using an inappropriate tone or inappropriate language

—pressing the send button without a quick edit and spellcheck

Request for Information

Subject
Announcement

Present
Circumstances

Conflict

Goodwill
Close

Etel, Adnan,

I need to know the financial projections for out-sourced production in the coming year.

Right now, I believe a 125% increase is authorized, although the previous projections held to 80%. The lower number is based on FIFO. The higher is LST.

I have no objection to 125% if Operations is comfortable. But I have just seen some correspondence suggesting that 125% is too high for Business to approve.

Please advise.

Regards,

Simone Fath
Associate Information Officer
Vector, Inc.
simonefath@vector.com

Tools

Use the "I" pronoun whenever you can

Many writers are anxious about using the "I" pronoun. At some point in their education, a teacher told them not to use it, and they've been trying to avoid the "I" pronoun ever since.

This is a big mistake! The "I" pronoun is standard in most business correspondence. Its use is encouraged.

The "I" pronoun usually speeds things up

Because the "I" pronoun puts you in the driver's seat, it often leads to clear, more vigorous sentence construction. Compare "The orders are currently being processed" to "I am processing the orders."

The "I" pronoun allows you to take credit

Often in business, it's preferable to own your work by directly stating your accomplishments. "I am processing the orders" gives you credit for the work you're doing. "The orders are currently being processed" certainly doesn't.

The "I" pronoun emphasizes the bond between the writer and reader

If there's an "I" who's writing, there has to be a "you" who's reading. The two pronouns go together. Emphasizing your business relationships through pronoun usage is a good way of reminding the reader that you're working together.

The "I" pronoun doesn't mean you're egotistical

Bilingual writers, or writers who have been educated outside of the United States, often feel as if using the "I" pronoun makes them look conceited. Nothing could be further from the truth.

The emphasis on individuality in the Anglophone world means that English language readers expect credit to be given where credit is due. If you are working on a particular project, say it straight out: "I am working on…"

A direct statement is always valued over a coy disclaimer. Downplaying your accomplishments in the hopes that someone else will recognize them usually doesn't work.

> **Use your time wisely**
> It's quicker to spend 5 extra minutes cleaning up a sloppy e-mail than it is to take time correcting misconceptions triggered by confused writing. A poorly written e-mail usually requires additional correspondence to clarify and correct what should have been clear the first time around.

*N*etiquette

Keep your e-mail tone informal and professional. Gone are the days when we elaborately greeted the reader using his or her title before getting to the point. Formulas such as, "In view of the following facts" and "Please allow me to draw your attention to," are simply not efficient. In today's climate, straightforward communication is prized because it saves time.

For this reason, you want to use clear vocabulary, rather than lofty vocabulary. You don't want to show-off, insist on your intellectual prowess, or appear to be putting on airs. Neither do you want to adopt an adolescent tone, using inappropriate SMS abbreviations, such as "u" instead of "you." Adolescents don't do business—professionals do, and they use a professional vocabulary. Casual slang and swear words are to be avoided for the same reasons.

The goal is to be friendly and straightforward. The people you do business with usually take for granted that you're a nice person who knows what you're doing. You can maintain that opinion simply by ensuring that your e-mails are direct and to the point.

*O*ptions

I need information about...

Please provide feedback on...

Could you please tell me...

What's the status/update on...

You might be able to help with...

I need to know...

Do you know...

I want to know...

Do you have details on...

Can I have your opinion...

Reply to a Request for Information

Subject Announcement

First Option

Second Option

Goodwill Close

Andrew, Sandy,

Here's the information you requested on the HSF alloy investment.

If we buy:

Optimistic figures on 7-year horizon suggest future cash inflows at about 78M. Low interest rates in Central America look stable, and the HR legislation that just passed gives management more latitude than in the past. It's not another SoCorp scenario.

If we don't buy:

The chief risk is that Lumina will make a move that will potentially increase competition in Central American markets. We can postpone investment until Reichart is on the block and then position for subsidiaries.

Give me a call before the week is up and we'll discuss the details.

Regards,

Karen Vormann
Financial Associate
Vector, Inc.
karenvormann@vector.com

Tools

Favor short e-mails over long ones whenever you can

Long e-mails take too much time to read. They're too hard on the eyes. They require more effort to get through. For these reasons, try to keep your e-mail to a laptop screen size whenever you can. The reader will appreciate it. And you'll have a better chance of zeroing in on the most important points.

Don't make the reader scroll

Scrolling takes extra keystrokes and extra time. If the reader has to scroll, you better make sure it's worthwhile.

For some e-mail, it's necessary. But much of the time, writers put in too much information and make the reader scroll through ideas that are either unnecessary or which belong elsewhere, perhaps in an attachment.

Consider divvying up a long e-mail into separate short e-mails

A reader would rather open up several short e-mails dedicated to different subjects than open one long e-mail that includes everything. The main points tend to get lost or blur in a long e-mail. In a short one, the odds are better that the information is clearly organized.

Don't put all the background info into an e-mail

Because e-mail lends itself to brevity, you should only put necessary information in an e-mail. Put lengthy background information in an attachment.

Recognize the link between brevity and confidence

In many firms, the more authority the writer has, the shorter his or her e-mails become. You have to put in enough information to get your point across, of course. But many writers are inclined to put in way too much. Detailing a subject to death makes you look unsure of your own opinions and authority.

Don't put everything in writing

Careful! Business insiders know that sensitive information either passes through the Legal Department or it's not written down!

Save the sensitive stuff for a phone call. Or, better yet, a face-to-face meeting. After all, you can't control who reads your e-mail, or where and when it might be forwarded.

Inbox

The boss says...

What is this person trying to say? • Can't they hire people who know how to write? • Why can't he use the spellchecker? • It's hard to figure out how someone as sharp as Pablo can write so poorly. • Hasn't anyone told her? • I though Elsa was the right one to fill the post, but after reading this doc, I'm not so sure. • We can't afford to give more authority to someone with poor writing skills. • Put this e-mail at the bottom of the pile, I don't have time to figure it out right now. • Can't any of them learn how to edit?

Advice

Business writers of every stripe often make the same mistake. They think that long, convoluted sentences and lofty vocabulary demonstrate intellectual sophistication and professional achievement. After all, they've spent a fortune on education. They've worked hard to expand their vocabulary. They've passed the SAT and maybe the GMAT. Maybe they've had to go to school at night instead of relaxing with family and friends; or maybe they had to work two jobs. They've studied hard. And the books they read in school used big words and complex sentences.

Therefore, big words and long, complex sentences suggest intellectual accomplishment.

In business email, nothing could be further from the truth. Big words and complex sentences belong to textbooks or hardcopy. They're made for reflection. A business email is different—it's a transaction. In one you reflect on information over time; in the other, you transact information from writer to reader.

Using long, complex sentences and lofty vocabulary doesn't further information exchange. Instead of hastening the process along, it slows it down or even stops it.

Consider, for a moment, writers who use words that they're not completely sure of. Often they don't even bother to look up the meanings—they just try them out in an e-mail to a colleague and hope for the best. Or they let their sentences run on and on in order to communicate the complexity of their thoughts. These writers think by borrowing a literary style—even one they don't fully understand—they show how smart they are.

Then there are the writers who have actually mastered a range of polysyllabic vocabulary and complex sentence structures. Often they use their knowledge to prove how educated and well-read they are, even if they suspect the reader won't understand. These writers are trying to show off and get attention by parading knowledge.

Both approaches are doomed to failure. Words and sentence structure belong to thought itself—you can't try them on or use them to impress your friends the way you do a platinum watch. Words must correctly fit the context, or they're of no use at all. In business e-mail, success is measured by clarity, not by literary pretension. Sometimes polysyllabic vocabulary and complex sentences might be desirable, but they're more rare than common.

Similarly, higher value is placed on a straightforward paragraph than one that resorts to literary affect. In a well-written paragraph, the first sentence usually tells the reader what the paragraph is about, and every other sentence in the paragraph supports the first sentence.

Your boss is often your editor

When e-mails are forwarded from one desk to another in a firm, they often have to be cleaned up. Worse yet, they have to be rewritten. Greater responsibility—and the higher paycheck that goes with it—has more to do with writing ability than is often acknowledged.

In the same way, the opening of an email immediately announces the subject that's discussed in the subsequent paragraphs. The opening of an email shouldn't mislead the reader, or try to dazzle him or her with suspense.

Business email is about transacting information as clearly, rapidly, and concisely as possible. For this reason, *a simple, direct statement is valued over other forms of expression.*

Do...

Choose clear and direct words.

Keep sentences short whenever possible.

Put the subject at the front of the sentence and follow it by the verb.

Encourage the reader with short paragraphs.

Don't...

Strive for vocabulary that is polysyllabic, lofty, inflated.

Mistake long sentences for sophisticated prose.

Put the subject and verb at the end of a sentence.

Forget that long paragraphs turn readers off.

Offload literary pretension into business e-mail.

A cautionary tale

"What do you want from me?" snapped the VP of a major international corporation on the phone. I was in Chicago; he was in Paris.

I was flabbergasted. "Well, I, uh, I...." All of a sudden it hit me: My e-mail hadn't been clear. He was obliged to call me to figure it out. I was wasting that man's precious time. I was wasting my own. I was wasting the company's. And from the tone in his voice, he knew it, too.

My survival instinct kicked in, and I quickly communicated the major points I thought I had covered in the e-mail. That experience taught me a key lesson about e-mail communication: Get the message across, right away.

CHAPTER TWO

Sharing Information

INCLUDING

For Your Information

Cover for Attached Document

Summary of a Conference Call

Announcement of a Meeting

Summary of a Meeting

Confirmation of an Oral Agreement

For Your Information

Subject
Announcement

First Outcome

Second Outcome

Goodwill
Close

Jenn,

This is just to tell you that I sent the budget to Lumina.

Sue signed off on it yesterday. In the cover letter we made it clear that we want written confirmation of the variance limits.

If they don't send it, I will inform them in writing that our projections will be used in future negotiations.

Based on our discussions, I think they'll send the variance report. But we'll see.

I'll keep you informed.

Regards,

Michelle Nollebaum
Assistant Budget Analyst
Vector, Inc.
michellenollebaum@vector.com

 Tools

Announce your FYI in the first sentence of the e-mail or bear the wrath!

While it's good to try and keep everyone informed of developments, it's not good to trick readers into reading an e-mail that doesn't require immediate attention. If you don't announce the FYI in the first sentence, odds are you're doing just that—tricking the reader into reading. The FYI subject line of the e-mail isn't enough. The busy reader may be opening mail in quick succession without even paying attention to the subject line. You have to alert the reader to the FYI in the first line of the body of the text.

Remember that e-mail is a synonym for action

Business professionals open e-mail to find out what action they have to take: make a decision, answer a question, right a situation, set up a face-to-face, review a draft, and so on. That means the reader is looking for what he or she has to *do*.

Because an FYI doesn't require action, it confuses readers if it's not labeled both in the subject line and in the first sentence of the e-mail. You don't want readers to try and decide what they're supposed to *do* when they read your e-mail, especially if the answer is nothing.

Use your judgment carefully in an FYI

As with those egregious e-mail chain letters that threaten bad luck if you don't forward the letter to six people in the next 10 minutes, FYIs require a judgment call. Sometimes, the information doesn't have to be forwarded at all.

The rapidity of e-mail encourages us to relay way too much information. Heaping your colleagues' inboxes with nonessential e-mail literally sends a message of immaturity. Seasoned colleagues use good judgment to draw the line between what keeps the boss informed and what wastes the boss's time.

Recognize that your FYI might not even be read

The busy reader with 200 e-mails in the inbox might delete your FYI after the first line, or file it to read later, if ever. An FYI is optional, not compulsory.

*O*ptions

FYI...   To make sure we're on the same page...

Heads up...   This is just to tell you...

This is to inform you...   For your information/files...

Just so you know...   I wanted to let you know that...

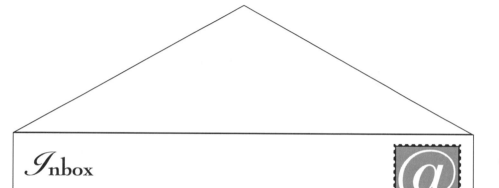

*I*nbox

How many times have I heard the following FYI complaints? Too many!

—I've got enough work to do. If I want to know that information, I'll ask for it!

—I spent all that time wading through the darn e-mail and then I find out it's superfluous!

—Nothing irritates me more than an FYI e-mail that's not prefaced as such. They waste time, energy, and disk space.

Cover for Attached Document

Subject Announcement

Summary of Document

Suggestions for Directed Reading

Goodwill Close

Laura,

I am pleased to attach the new HR final report, "Spark Commitment: IT and Vector Employees."

Authored by Lanten and Associates, the report explains how IT can strengthen the link between employee motivation and productivity in every function. Information bonds, for example, are often overlooked in our business culture. Viewing the employee's intellectual property in emotive as well as rational terms enhances dedication. And dedication to the company leads to results.

I would specifically like to draw your attention to the section on Vector E-mail Policy (VEP). As you know, policy discussions are heating up in the next quarter. I will be interested in hearing your thoughts about the report's findings at the next VEP meeting.

Please let me know what you think when you get a chance.

Regards,
Frances Ventoux
HR Associate
Vector Affiliate Action Group
francesventoux@vector.com

Tools

Tell the reader why the attached document is of interest

"Please find attached" doesn't always suffice! Sometimes the content of the attachment is enough to compel the reader to open the attachment right away—if the reader is waiting for it. But in other situations, you need to persuade the reader to actually skim the attachment—or to even print it out for slow and careful consideration.

Include a sentence or short paragraph highlighting the relevance of the attachment

Readers want to know "why"—why they're reading the e-mail, why they're going to open the attachment, and why they'll find it worthwhile. The trick here is to appeal to the reader's self-interest. Take a moment to quickly explain to him or her how, exactly, they'll profit from reading your document. If you can phrase your sentence(s) so that it looks as if you're doing the reader a favor—"if you read this attachment thoroughly, you'll look good at the meeting"—all the better.

Suggest that the reader is accountable for feedback

Politely telling the readers that you're looking forward to their feedback on a particular attachment is a good way to emphasize accountability. If you can pinpoint a deadline for the feedback, say, at the next meeting, your request looks even more serious. That way, you're not simply forwarding an attachment to an inbox—the reader is expected to look at the attachment and have something to say. Busy readers who can't get to it will honestly tell you so, while the foot-draggers will either have come up with an excuse to save face or actually do the reading.

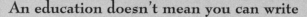

An education doesn't mean you can write

Business professionals with impressive educational credentials can still have trouble communicating. Business professionals with a modest educational background can sometimes communicate very well. It's more or less the luck of the draw if you had a writing teacher who pushed you in the right direction, or one who cramped your abilities for years on end.

Suggest a specific part of the document for the reader to focus on and explain why

You can take some of the pressure off the reader by offering a directed reading. He or she doesn't have to trudge through the whole thing, only the bits that are the most relevant. Making a directed-reading move in a cover letter suggests you recognize how valuable the reader's time is, and that you don't want to waste it.

*N*etiquette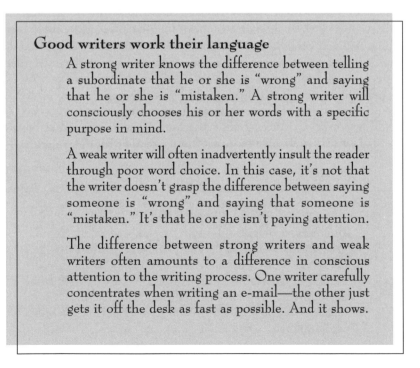

Always remember that your e-mail has unseen readers. Once information is digital, it's durable—and you have no real control over where it goes or who sees it. Your e-mail may be forwarded immediately—or in the future— to people you don't know or whom you'll never meet. The forwards may be accidental, intentional, or the result of subterfuge. But it all adds up to one thing: Privacy is not assured, and confidentiality is always at risk. If you're not comfortable with others reading your e-mail, think twice about sending it.

Good writers work their language

A strong writer knows the difference between telling a subordinate that he or she is "wrong" and saying that he or she is "mistaken." A strong writer will consciously chooses his or her words with a specific purpose in mind.

A weak writer will often inadvertently insult the reader through poor word choice. In this case, it's not that the writer doesn't grasp the difference between saying someone is "wrong" and saying that someone is "mistaken." It's that he or she isn't paying attention.

The difference between strong writers and weak writers often amounts to a difference in conscious attention to the writing process. One writer carefully concentrates when writing an e-mail—the other just gets it off the desk as fast as possible. And it shows.

Summary of a Conference Call

Subject Announcement

Declaration

Subject Area

Facts

Subject Area

Facts

Goodwill Close

Zara, Norm, Carla,

The April 18, 2007 conference call on the LITE deal included: one Lumina partner, one Rawls partner, and the Vector team (Langston from Corporate Tax, Duncan from Operations Management and myself).

We agreed to the following:

Corporate Structure

1. Vector will sell its shares in LITE Consulting directly to Lumina on the day of closing.

2. Audit partners will receive their consideration in cash.

3. Consulting Partners will receive deferred consideration consisting of three yearly installments paid in Lumina shares.

Further Observations

1. Because Lumina owns the shares upon closing, the new company can integrate immediately.

2. Although state law prohibits acquisition of the parent company's shares, in this case, we're not infringing on restrictions since shares will be used as a payment for the transaction.

We have another phone call scheduled with LITE tomorrow. Let me know if I can supply additional information.

Regards,

Ron Kocik
Mergers and Acquisitions Associate
Vector, Inc.
ronkocik@vector.com

 *Tools*

Don't clutter your e-mail with an elaborate outline system

Nobody wants to confront a list of I, A, 2, c, or iv in an e-mail. A system that combines Roman and Arabic numbers, and upper and lower case figures and letters is too visually complicated and too cumbersome on a screen. These old-fashioned outline systems are often confined to attached contracts, policies, and other legal documents. But even here, the trend in attachments is to simplify the numeric system whenever possible.

Choose simple, sequential numbers to organize your points

Numeric systems are meant to order information, not steal the show. It's better to opt for a straightforward numbering system that provides structure, rather than using a more complicated system that draws attention to itself.

Follow the number by a right parenthesis, such as 1), 2), and so on. Or use the number followed by a period, such as 1., 2., and 3. Avoid more fussy or complicated methods, such as: 1/, 1) -, or (1.).

Arabic numbers are favored in business; Roman numerals are usually reserved for more formal content. In an everyday business e-mail, Roman numerals risk appearing conservative or old-fashioned.

Decide the sequence

Sometime the most important point goes first. Other times, you may want to simply list the points chronologically in the order that they were made. If you are *recounting* events that took place at a meeting, chronology is the logical method to use. But if you're *summarizing* what happened at a meeting, prioritizing the points in terms of importance—1 being the most important—is the best option.

Announcement of a Meeting

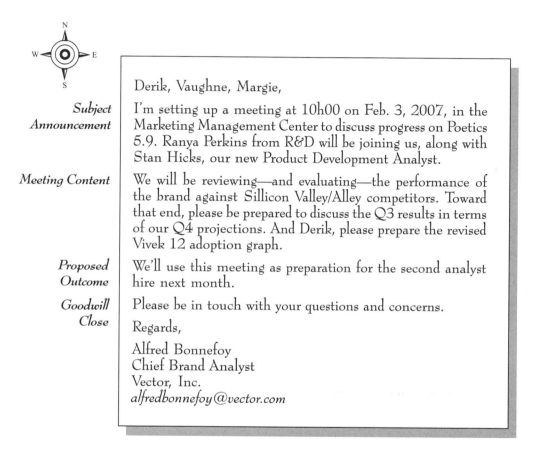

Subject Announcement

Derik, Vaughne, Margie,

I'm setting up a meeting at 10h00 on Feb. 3, 2007, in the Marketing Management Center to discuss progress on Poetics 5.9. Ranya Perkins from R&D will be joining us, along with Stan Hicks, our new Product Development Analyst.

Meeting Content

We will be reviewing—and evaluating—the performance of the brand against Sillicon Valley/Alley competitors. Toward that end, please be prepared to discuss the Q3 results in terms of our Q4 projections. And Derik, please prepare the revised Vivek 12 adoption graph.

Proposed Outcome

We'll use this meeting as preparation for the second analyst hire next month.

Goodwill Close

Please be in touch with your questions and concerns.

Regards,

Alfred Bonnefoy
Chief Brand Analyst
Vector, Inc.
alfredbonnefoy@vector.com

Tools

Don't forget the logistics!

Although it sounds too obvious to mention, many writers neglect one or more of the who, when, where, what, and why details when announcing a meeting. The reader has to request more information via e-mail, and the writer has to write one or more e-mails to clarify information that should have been clear in the first place.

A pattern of neglecting simple, straightforward information is a sure way of supplying proof that you're disorganized. Or that you're too distracted to pay attention to the task that's in front of you. Or that you don't review and revise your own e-mail!

Put logistic details in the order of importance

If everyone has to travel to a distant city, the "where" of the meeting might take precidence. If the participants frequently work off-site, the "when" might be more important. If it's more or less sure everyone is going to be at the home office, then the time of the meeting might be the primary concern.

Because the sequence of information often determines emphasis in English, lead with the most important detail for your audience.

Choose the time abbreviation suited to your firm and context

Is it a ten o'clock meeting? (No, it's old-fashioned.)

10 am? (No, "am" looks like a verb.)

Ten? (No, because we routinely use Roman numbers, not English words, for time.)

10 a.m.? (This is acceptable.)

10? (Maybe, but it might be too casual for some firms or positions.)

10h00 GMT? (Maybe, but you only use time-zone abbreviations for appointments in which time zones matter.)

10:00? (This is acceptable if there's no risk of a.m./p.m. confusion.)

10h00? (This is acceptable if the firm uses a 24-hour clock.)

Choose the date abbreviation suited to your firm and context

Is it 3 Feb. 2006? (Yes, if you're not based in the United States or if you don't work for a U.S. company.)

February 3, 2006? (Doubtful, because long months are routinely abbreviated unless the document is formal.)

2/3/06? (Yes, assuming the order of the day and the month is clear.)

Feb. 3? (This is good, but firms or writing contexts that insist on formality will also insist on including the year.)

To be safe, choose the time and date abbreviations used by the firm in official correspondence

Oftentimes, writing decisions you're mulling over are already made for you. All it takes is one look at the annual report, a recent statement by the Big Boss, or a quick check of edited documents on the intranet, and it's figured out. If the boss uses the 24-hour clock, you should, too.

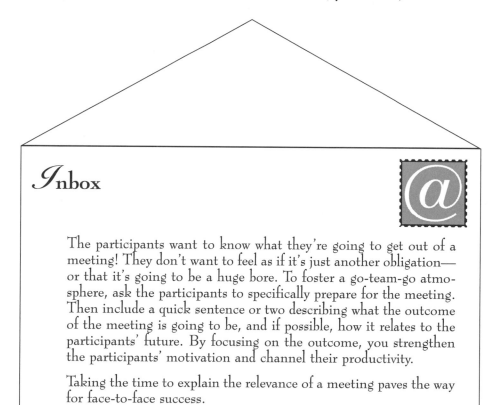

*I*nbox

The participants want to know what they're going to get out of a meeting! They don't want to feel as if it's just another obligation—or that it's going to be a huge bore. To foster a go-team-go atmosphere, ask the participants to specifically prepare for the meeting. Then include a quick sentence or two describing what the outcome of the meeting is going to be, and if possible, how it relates to the participants' future. By focusing on the outcome, you strengthen the participants' motivation and channel their productivity.

Taking the time to explain the relevance of a meeting paves the way for face-to-face success.

Summary of a Meeting

George,

Subject Announcement

Here are the notes from the March 8, 2007 Business Unit meeting at Vector HQ with Roberto, Kathy, Mateo, Mei and Ana.

Topic 1

1) Mateo questioned the date when the 35/45 arrangement will expire. Vector needs to clarify. <u>Action: Roberto.</u>

Topic 2

2) Mateo also asked whether Vector has any other clients in the same boat. If so, what plans are in place for them? <u>Action: Roberto.</u>

Topic 3

3) Lumina needs to confirm plans/progress on the Poetics upgrade at de Bracy. <u>Action: Mei.</u>

Topic 4

4) M&G Corp will propose dates for Rony and Anders to visit the Steiner Center. <u>Action: Ana to contact.</u>

Topic 5

5) We all agreed that the technical issues associated with migration from BJH suggested a disruption risk to Vector business. The migration timeline could exacerbate the situation. <u>Action: All will investigate minimizing risk.</u>

Regards,

Michael Palter
Business Unit Assistant
Vector, Inc.
michaelpalter@vector.com

*T*ools

Include the date in the message summarizing a call or a meeting

You may be tempted to say "yesterday's call," "today's call," or "last week's meeting." After all, there's a date stamp on the e-mail—that's enough, right? No, it's not. The reader might not pay attention to the date stamp in the e-mail, and have to click back to find it.

Even more importantly, if the e-mail is forwarded, copied, and/or printed, the date stamp risks being altered. This can lead to disaster if, in the future, the e-mail turns out to be important in establishing a chronology of events. Having the date in the body of the e-mail is just a little extra insurance that the meeting is properly contextualized.

List the people taking part in a call or in a meeting

Writing "Finance Department" doesn't suffice—not everyone might be there, and the members of the department change over time. You can list the attendees by name. If your firm maintains a more formal e-mail style, you may want to list their titles, too.

Time often plays funny tricks on us, so that we think we'll remember information that we don't. Memory dims quickly. All the more reason to quickly jot down the players so that you—or someone else—doesn't get caught out.

Add an action point to each topic of your meeting memo

Action points ensure that a job is done. Or at least, they provide a record of who didn't follow through!

Use the action point to close each topic, designate responsibility, describe a course of action, or promote progress. Visually emphasize the action point with italics, bold, or underlining.

Consider action points as motivational tools

The employee who sees his or her name assigned to a particular task in an e-mail circulated among colleagues is apt to complete the task. The employee who is told verbally to complete a task in a group setting can always maintain that he or she misunderstood.

Putting names and assignments in writing increases their formality. Why? Because the mere fact of writing something down makes it official. Although not all written records have the full force of the law behind them, the existence of documentation lends weight and creditability to the contents.

Options

Here are my notes…

Please find below the notes…

I hope you'll take time to review the notes…

Please take time to consider the notes…

Would you take a moment to look over the notes…

The notes from the March 8 Business Unit meeting include…

I wanted to get the March 8 Business Unit notes to you as soon as possible…

What's a professional writer?

Journalists are usually thought of as professional writers. So are novelists and screenwriters. And the technical writers who pen the directions for our cake mixes and write the brochures for our hotels are pros, too. But there is another kind of professional writer— the one in business who has to write at work, the one with 50, 150, or 500 e-mails in the inbox every day.

If we define a professional writer by the number of hours spent reading and writing per day, then many business workers across all sectors can claim to be professional writers. These in-house writers should know the shortcuts, just like other writing professionals. Instead of trying to wing it, they should have a clear understanding of the goals of effective e-mail communication. They should have a range of simple writing strategies that work.

Confirmation of an Oral Agreement

Subject
Announcement

Fact

Opinion

Goodwill
Close

Jo, Don,

This is to confirm that I have understood our Sept. 8, 2007 conversation.

Due to uptake problems in the forward quadrants, the rollout schedule for Poetics 5.9 has been revised. Follow-up testing is scheduled at weekly intervals throughout the fall. R&D is working with the Poetics team to resolve manufacturing problems, but there won't be a hard update until all the data is in.

In my opinion, we need to contact C&N about renegotiating outsourcing in the event of further delay.

Let me know if this is right, and I'll organize a meeting for the week of Sept. 12.

Regards,

Kitty Okamurra
Assistant Director of Manufacturing
Vector, Inc.
kittyokamurra@vector.com

$\mathscr{T}$ools

Confirm oral information whenever it's appropriate

In busy offices, important information is as likely to be exchanged in an elevator as in a conference room. Don't make the mistake of thinking your interlocutors will remember your conversation—oftentimes, they don't! You may forget the details, too. Keeping records of an oral exchange is vital in terms of protecting your position. In the casual business idiom, this strategy is called "Cover Your Ass" or "CYA."

Emphasize the facts

Whenever you confirm oral information, think of the document you're writing as a kind of transcript. You don't have to catch every nuance of a conversational exchange, but you do have to summarize in your own words what you heard and said. Note who was present, mention specific dates whenever possible, list any requests for action, and any agreements. If an issue has been left hanging or is undecided, mention that, too.

Divide facts from opinions

Objectivity is comforting in the business world! If you follow up a paragraph of facts with a paragraph of opinion, the reader will be inclined to listen to your point of view.

But if you mix facts and opinions, you may be headed for trouble. Bouncing back and forth between the two puts stress on your transitions so that the writing is more difficult to control. You may be tempted to compromise clarity. Worse yet, you may also send the message that you can't draw the line between what is happening in the business and how you feel about it.

Don't write anything down you're not supposed to

Sensitive information is confined to oral communications in a firm. Because of potential legal risks, some information never makes it to the hard drive. If you're ever in doubt about the nature of the information you're documenting, ask before you put it down.

*N*etiquette

Business e-mail frowns on emotional frills. No more "Hello, how are you today?" or "I really hope this e-mail finds you well and thriving." These kinds of friendly markers may still appear in personal e-mail, but they're usually a waste of time in the business world.

Interestingly enough, the suppression of friendly markers—everything from the "Hi there" in the opening to the "Let's get together" in the close—isn't perceived as rude, cold, or even unfriendly.

The emphasis in business e-mail is on the facts, not on warm-and-fuzzy relationships between colleagues. Because team spirit, mutual respect, and good working relationships are usually required, they aren't continually reinforced in writing. The "Goodwill Close" is enough to ensure camaraderie. A straightforward, factual tone sends the message that you're a reliable employee, while too many emotional words and phrases might bring your work, as well as your character, into question.

*O*ptions

This is to confirm...

In my opinion...

It seems to me that...

In my view...

My thoughts about this...

My position is that...

From my perspective...

Perhaps we should...

The history suggests...

If you ask me...

Instinct tells me that...

Similar situations have shown...

It makes sense to me that...

I wonder if...

It occurs to me that...

My experience suggests...

I believe that...

My stand is...

> ## Written communication skills get noticed
>
> Many writers over the years have proudly told me how they've been complimented at work on their e-mail documents. These same writers were once singled out for their poor communication skills. Not anymore. Writers who sharpen their skills are often recognized by management. They prove that effort does, indeed, lead to improvement in writing, as well as in other areas.

Advice

To jargon or not to jargon

Every sector, business, firm, function, department, and even some cohort teams have a specific vocabulary used on the job. This specialized vocabulary is called "jargon" and includes slang, abbreviations, acronyms, and technical terms.

For example, M&A (Mergers and Acquisitions) is a common abbreviation used by business professionals around the world. But the acronym EMEA (Europe, Middle East, Asia) might be arcane for an employee in Brazil. Similarly, GNP (Gross National Product) is common, LIFO (Last In, First Out) less so, and D2E (debt to equity ratio) is mostly confined to the accounting department.

For years, business communication specialists argued against jargon in any form. Why? Because if the reader doesn't share the jargon, you're not communicating. When this happens, you have to write a second (and perhaps even a third) e-mail, saying what you could have said clearly the first time around—if only you'd dropped the jargon and used common words.

More recently, the wholesale dismissal of jargon has yielded to a kinder, gentler position toward insider vocabulary. Here's why: it saves time. If I can write "SG&A" in an e-mail instead of "Selling, General, and Administrative Expense" and still get the same concept across, I'm communicating more rapidly and efficiently. And if I can use several acronyms in an e-mail, I've saved a lot of time.

But concision is not the only reason why communication professionals have relaxed their stand on jargon. Another reason is that it continues to multiply. Rather than going away—as some writers had hoped—jargon has become an essential part of our intellectual property. It takes a long time to learn it, and even longer to feel comfortable with it. Instead of confusing readers, jargon can have the opposite effect; it can reinforce professional know-how and relationships.

Jargon is the marker of selective inclusion. If you think of it as a kind of secret language, known only to the initiated, jargon sets a standard, dividing who's in from who's out. Those who know the jargon belong to the club, those who don't remain outside.

Sharing a secret language has a long history in human relationships. Mothers and children, for example, often have pet names, families use special made-up terms, and even corporate firms have their own insider endearments. In every case, secret language reinforces human bonds. Using jargon appropriately on the job underscores the fact that you're a player. But deciding *if* and *when* to use business jargon is tricky.

For example, I recently received an e-mail from a large international corporation that told me to "upload the WP at W3 with the IA." Worse yet, I was told to do it right away! Because I had no idea what a "WP" was, let alone a "W3" or an "IA," I had to write back saying that I didn't understand. This led to further complications. Eventually—several e-mails later—I was able to execute the task.

This experience underscores the problem: Jargon isn't the issue; the audience is. Other correspondents would have immediately understood what the jargon in my e-mail meant. In other words, the main issue with jargon is not the growing number of acronyms and abbreviations—it's choosing the reader.

Insider words, used inappropriately, can arouse feelings of frustration, inadequacy, and even anger. In the worse case scenario, jargon can be used on purpose to alienate readers. A seasoned employee, passed up for a promotion, might deluge the new hire with jargon in a doomed bid to assert his or her authority. Or a supervisor may use jargon unfamiliar to employees in order to emphasize that they should do their homework.

Some companies place jargon dictionaries on their intranets to help new employees get up to speed. Often colleagues will also help fill in the blanks. Using jargon wisely and correctly reinforces self-confidence and membership in the group. Just keep in mind who you're writing to.

Do...

Use jargon with other professionals—those with whom you work closely.

Remember that using jargon appropriately will save you time.

Don't...

Use jargon with those outside the inner circle of colleagues.

Confuse jargon with inflated vocabulary or wordiness. No one likes that.

Writing your way up the ladder

The ability to write crisp, clear, and clean e-mail can result in raises and promotions. But lack of writing ability can stall out a career. Or even end it.

Chapter Three

Delicate Situations

Including

Request for Special Treatment

Problem-Solving Suggestion

Reassigning Fault

Retroactive Correction

Misplaced Document

Refusal to Participate

Apology for Inappropriate Behavior

Request for Special Treatment

Subject Announcement

Request for Special Treatment

Reason 1

Reason 2

Conclusion

Goodwill Close

Mira,

I am writing with regard to the Vector Audit Team visit to Industrial Sales, scheduled on June 14 at 8:00 a.m.

I know from the advance schedule that Audit has a tight program. I also know that the time slots for various departments were confirmed weeks ago. But if we can push back the date, it would be to our mutual advantage.

Here's why: I have just received word that two of our Sales Directors will be negotiating an important cross-sell deal during the same window.

We can go ahead with the meeting if there is no other option. But I feel certain that productivity will be enhanced if we have a 100% attendance rate. We can reduce the workload of post-meeting follow-up if our top directors are included.

I thought it was worthwhile to run the idea past you.

I look forward to hearing from you soon.

Regards,

Forrester Evans
Applied Industrial Sales
Vector, Inc.
forresterevans@vector.com

Tools

When making a preferential request, acknowledge the reader's resistance

Generally speaking, people don't like to make plans and then change them because of someone else's needs. It makes more work. Besides, you should have spoken up earlier, when things were in the planning stage.

Showing your reader that you *know* you're asking for special treatment may increase the reader's beneficence. Some writers might even go so far as to express regret—but be careful! It's easier to reject someone who is groveling, who knows that he or she is in the wrong, than it is someone who looks you in the eye with a straightforward request.

Make the request right away

Stalling the request or mincing words won't result in sympathy for your position. It will have the opposite effect—frustrating and irritating the reader. Say what you have to say straight out, without apology.

Insist on the benefits, not the inconveniences

Don't dwell on the problems you're causing—that only adds fuel to the fire. Instead, try and draw attention to the positive outcomes you hope to achieve. Rephrase negative ideas in a positive way. Instead of "Our Sales Directors will be unable to attend the meeting," try "Our Sales Directors will be negotiating an important cross-sell deal."

Immediately explain the reasoning behind the request

The more your reasoning benefits the reader, the more likely you'll win your case. It's to your advantage to show how both parties will profit from the change.

Notice the differences

Good writers can instantly judge whether an e-mail is effective or a waste a time. Professional writers can actually tell you *why* one e-mail is better than another. But many poor writers don't notice differences in quality. Learning to recognize a successful e-mail is the first step toward writing one.

Confine negative information to dependent clauses

English language readers unconsciously emphasize the main clause of a sentence—that's where the action is. The dependent clause is just the set-up, where contextualizing information goes. Consequently, you can downplay negative information just by shunting it off into a dependent clause. For example, put "If we can push back the date" in the dependent clause, and save the positive stuff for the main clause, "it will be to our mutual advantage."

Leave the ball in the reader's court

You never want to insist on special treatment—at least in the early rounds! Readers who feel that their authority is being recognized are generally sympathetic to requests. After all, it allows them to act with largesse. But readers who feel they are being pressured (or even forced) to make a change generally increase their resistance.

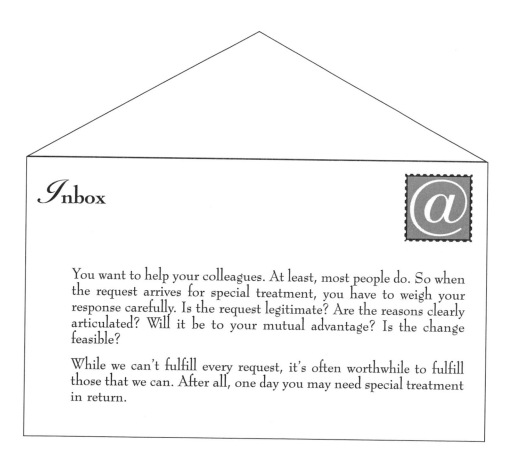

*I*nbox

You want to help your colleagues. At least, most people do. So when the request arrives for special treatment, you have to weigh your response carefully. Is the request legitimate? Are the reasons clearly articulated? Will it be to your mutual advantage? Is the change feasible?

While we can't fulfill every request, it's often worthwhile to fulfill those that we can. After all, one day you may need special treatment in return.

Problem-Solving Suggestion

Berri,

Subject
Announcement

I'd like to suggest we solve the backlog of photocopying by Web scheduling copy time until the new scanners arrive.

Explicit Problem

I think you might agree that everyone in Assets & Liabilities is aware of the backlog problem. We've nearly all had to wait to photocopy. Some of us get there early; some of us stay late. We've even had to go back and forth between our desks and the machine, hoping for an opportunity.

Implicit Problem

But it's not simply a problem of logistics. The fact that we have to interrupt work to position ourselves at the machine impacts our productivity. Frankly, I believe that concern about how and when to photocopy documents takes on greater importance than it should.

Solution

We could possibly alleviate the situation if we posted a virtual sign-up sheet on the site. Photocopying time could be scheduled in half-hour increments. We could leave an open hour at the beginning and end of the day for emergencies or for unexpected tasks. That way, we'd lose less time going back and forth between our desks and standing around waiting.

Goodwill
Close

Let me know if you think my suggestion could work.

Regards,

Kate Kennings
Assistant Assets Analyst
Vector, Inc.
katekennings@vector.com

*T*ools

Don't mistake giving an order with making a suggestion!

Sometimes enthusiasm or frustration gets the better of us. We sound bossy, when really we only want to be supportive. The difference between bossy language and suggestive language is often just a matter of degree. For example, replacing "You will agree" with "You might agree" is enough to take the edge off.

Try to point out that the problem is a shared concern

The last thing you want to do is single yourself out as a complainer! If the problem is yours, then it's usually yours to deal with, too.

But if the problem affects others, explain how and why. Show concern for the impact on the group. Better yet, identify a solution. In doing so, you reinforce your status as a good team player. You're acting not only to save yourself irritation and inconvenience, but you're also working to help your colleagues.

Emphasize that the reader understands the issues

You score points by giving the reader credit for recognizing the problem— even when he or she is apparently oblivious to the issue! The bigger the boss, the more their eyes are on the big picture. The details aren't always in focus—unless someone calls attention to them.

Flattery goes a long way. Don't ever assume the boss hasn't noticed something. On the contrary, always assume that he or she has. Your confidence in the boss's capabilities will get you at least a hearing. It might even help you solve the problem.

Use the "we" pronoun whenever possible

"We" refers to the reader and writer, of course. A "we" can't be adversarial. It is, by nature, united. A deft use of "we" underscores that you're on the same team and working together. You're not a complainer—heaven forbid!—you're a proactive, self-starting, problem-solver. And using "we" helps bring that message home.

Opt for tentative language

Modal verbs, such as "might" and "could," along with qualifiers such as "possibly" and "probably," put the ball in the reader's court. You want to guide the reader to take a particular course of action, not force him or her into a corner.

The writer you want to be is more important than the writer you are

Most people have had bad writing experiences at one time or another. Some people are haunted by those experiences. Some folks have even been traumatized by them. The idea that "I can't write well" becomes a self-fulfilling prophecy. Thinking in this way will not help you advance in your career. Everyone of normal intelligence can learn to communicate effectively in e-mail.

Netiquette

E-mail favors contractions. Because e-mail is direct and informal, contractions are encouraged. "I'll," "he's," "we're," and so on are par for the course. Contractions emphasize, through their informality, the camaraderie of good business colleagues. Moreover, contractions save time. A few nanoseconds of cognitive expenditure are saved when we read or write "she'd" instead of "she would." And in business, we need every neural increment we can get!

But there are, however, specific cases when writers opt for whole words rather than contractions. Official business documents, such as a reprimand for an employee's file, or most legal documents, require greater formality, using whole words instead of contractions. We also prefer to write out contractions when we want to emphasize the negative thrust in a statement. "He will not" is more negative than "he won't." Similarly, "She would prefer" is more emphatic than "she'd prefer."

Be careful, though, of the temptation of foregoing contractions altogether. Why? Because beginning writers, inexperienced writers, and nonnative speakers of English routinely contract less in writing than experienced English language writers. Contractions are associated with fluency and style; a lack of contractions is associated with language difficulties.

One way of checking for contractions is to read the e-mail aloud. Writers who speak in contractions, but don't write with them, can easily improve their e-mail style simply by listening to their own speech.

Reassigning Fault

Subject
Announcement

Admission

Explanation

Reassignment
of Fault

Goodwill
Close

Doug,

Thank you for your e-mail supplying evidence that the GS6 Factor Emollient is not binding in Fork 8 Upgrade testing.

As GS6 Factor Supervisor, I personally verified the binding data before we shipped. It appears, however, that the Lumina lab providing the base emulsion complex is experiencing data-corruption problems.

The thickening agent is not consistently performing to standards. Consequently, the base emulsion complex is subject to rapid deterioration at temperatures inferior to 3C. Our GS6 lab, as you know, does not test in these conditions.

Because our lab cannot be responsible for conditions we are unable to test for, I suggest you contact Joe Perkins, Director of Quality Control at Lumina, to arrange this matter. His e-mail is *jperkins@lumina.com*.

If I can assist you further, please let me know.

Regards,

Maria Houtling
GS6 Factor Supervisor
Vector, Inc.
mariahoutling@vector.com

 *Tools*

When dealing with a complaint, be thankful that it was brought to your attention

Taking a defensive tack makes you look guilty and unsure. It also makes you look like you're at fault. If your conscious is clear, you probably won't feel insulted. You'll be grateful that someone has brought a problem to your attention.

Therefore, thank your interlocutor right off the bat! You want to set the stage for effective communication, not shut it down. Toward that end, keep a polite, neutral tone. Don't wallow in guilt, but don't insist on your innocence, either.

When there's an error or a problem, admit it

The best way to neutralize a complainer—or a potentially aggressive interlocutor—is to admit there's at least a grain of truth in his or her point of view. It takes the wind right out of their sails. Readers will be inclined to listen if you seem to be sympathetic to their position.

If, on the other hand, you're too angry or irritated to acknowledge at least a vestige of legitimacy in the complaint, prepare for another assault. Somebody who takes the time to complain is usually someone who won't give up.

Provide a rational explanation for redirecting responsibility

In order to get the reader off your back, you have to provide reasons why a particular problem is not your responsibility. The more specific and concrete the reasons, the more convincing they are.

Include a suggestion for further action

The person who has taken the time to complain to you about a problem deserves something in return. Saying that the problem is not your responsibility isn't enough—it's a letdown when the reader was hoping for a climax.

To maintain good working relationships, you have to make a useful suggestion. Give the name and contact information of someone else who might be able to help. You may want to forward the e-mail yourself. If you don't know who is the right person to deal with the problem, offer a method of finding out.

Taking a little extra time to show that you care about the outcome of the problem earns you a lot of points. And in business, where personal relationships count far more than is often recognized, having a few more good points on your tally sheet may be important to your future. You never know who is going to come back to haunt you—or help you—on your way.

*I*nbox

If you're pointing out that you've been wronged, more than anything else you want to be understood! You want to be acknowledged. You want a sympathetic ear. You want clear signals that your idea, complaint, suggestion, or accusation has been heard.

That's why conceding the legitimacy of the reader's position is crucial, even when you would rather press the delete button and get on with your life. Grit your teeth, thank the reader, and acknowledge his or her claim. Show you care. Then when you deny your responsibility, there's greater likelihood that you'll be heard.

Retroactive Correction

Subject
Announcement

Original
Information

Revised
Information

Quick
Regret

Goodwill
Close

Xavier,

New information has come to light regarding the sale and use of Datamax.

I was correct in stating that the Malaysian student may take the Datamax course offered by Vector—as long as course materials are public domain.

But it has come to my attention that:

- the student cannot have a current or prior association with the Malaysian government or with defense contractors;

- European subsidiaries are not in a position to provide technical support;

- the student is prohibited by law from U.S. support (including troubleshooting).

Therefore, the student will be in possession of products for which there is no available support whatsoever.

Furthermore, Cheryl rightly pointed out that there might be downstream policy reasons to retard the sale and use of Datamax in Malaysia. Revelations of the availability of Datamax in that country could cause negative publicity for the company, especially in the US.

Although the student may fulfill the conditions required to matriculate into the course, we want to steer clear of any future complications. I regret I didn't have this information earlier.

I'll let you know if the situation changes.

Regards,

Sharon Farmer
Cross-Border Oversight
Vector, Inc
sharonfarmer@vector.com

ℐools

Admit you made a mistake

You want to immediately alert the reader to the fact that you've got newer, better information. You don't want to emphasize that you didn't do your job properly or that you made a mistake—at least not right away!

Choose a phrase such as, "It has come to my attention," or "New information has come to light" instead of "Sorry, I have just realized that" or "Oops! I made a mistake..." By censuring the "I," you depersonalize the admission of error.

Emphasize what was right in your information before correcting what was wrong

You want to remind the reader what you got right before you lay out the corrected information. Use phrases such as "I was justified in saying...," "I was in the right when I...," or "My understanding of...was correct." That way you contextualize the negative in the positive. As much as possible, you want the misinformation to seem minor.

Lay out the corrected information without apology

Maintain a clear, authoritative tone—even if the mistake is a big one. The trick here is to try to separate the information from your feelings. The reader probably doesn't care about how you feel. He or she just wants correct information in order to proceed to the next task.

Give credit where credit is due

If a coworker has brought new information to light, credit him or her. You'll score points for your thoroughness and for your team spirit. Some writers make a mistake in thinking that withholding credit makes them look smarter. This is just plain wrong.

Business involves working well together with others. Don't forgo an opportunity to reaffirm your commitment to the group over and above personal gain. On the other hand, omitting (or even refusing) to acknowledge where the information came from can lead to distrust and resentment. The more confidant the writer, the more apt he or she is to give credit to others.

Include a polite statement of regret if it's appropriate

Including a quick regret at the end of your e-mail is polite. By acknowledging that you were wrong, you reinforce your honesty. You also show consideration for others who acted on your misinformation.

Misplaced Document

Subject
Announcement

Problem

Solution

Robert,

Denise asked me to send you the note on the HR matter we discussed earlier today.

Due to technical difficulties, I cannot access the document at present.

I will consult my hard copy files in order to locate a copy and get back to you before the close of the workday.

Regards,

Jes Chun
Assistant to the Business Unit Manager
Vector, Inc.
jeschun@vector.com

*T*ools

Admit you can't find the document right away

Given the volume of e-mail that's in the inbox, a lost document now and then isn't surprising. Computers crash, bringing the files down with them. Viruses colonize the hard disk. And a stressed employee might make a mistake under pressure, deleting a file instead of backing it up. Or an employee might be so overworked that he or she mislabels a file and can't find it again—at least, right away.

Get over the fact that a lost document is embarrassing and just deal with it. As long as it happens only once in a while, and not continually, your readers will be more sympathetic than accusatory. After all, they lose a document now and then, too.

Assure the reader that you'll solve the problem

Because we all make mistakes, we're usually reasonably sympathetic to human error in others, provided it doesn't occur on a regular basis. Reassuring the reader that you're fixing the situation is halfway to recovery.

Include a precise deadline for an update

Knowing that information is forthcoming mollifies a potentially irritated reader. Just make sure that if you promise to get back to a reader by such-and-such a time, that you actually do it. Otherwise, everything else you say you're doing will come into question, too.

Get help organizing your files if you often lose or misplace docs

The internal support offices in your firm should have ideas to help you. There's no shame in asking for technical help, but it's not a good idea to pretend you don't need it.

*N*etiquette

Business e-mail is suited to a short paragraph. But you may have been taught otherwise. Look at it this way: Once upon a time there was an idea that a paragraph should be some sort of text block. It was chunky. It was weighty. Some grammarians maintained that it had to have at least seven sentences. It had meat. It had to take up space. And it still does—in literature, journalism, and personal correspondence. It also shows up frequently in attachments. But it's rare in business e-mail. In business e-mail, a paragraph can look like this:

OK.

Or like this:

FYI.

Or even this:

No.

In other words, the normative paragraph in a business e-mail has slimmed down. It's gotten tighter and faster. Most importantly, the e-mail paragraph is made for skimming. The increase in white space and the trend toward headers reduces eyestrain, boosts reading speed, and favors comprehension.

No so with a thick and heavy text block! A chunky paragraph is made for reflection—the reader will take time to read it, reflect on it, think about it. The e-mail paragraph is suited to transaction, not reflection. The idea is to transact information from writer to reader.

Because it's complements the rapidity of medium, the short paragraph performs better. Writers who compose in short paragraphs are forced to pay more attention to the structure of their prose. They're also less apt to default into the so-called "stream of consciousness" mode or resort to a defensive or unconscious repetition of word, sentence, and idea. Save your impressive, traditional paragraphs for the attachments or your literary activities. Prefer the shorter, faster paragraph in your business e-mail.

Refusal to Participate

Subject
Announcement

Praise

Refusal

Goodwill
Close

Ed, Jean, Lorna, Anne,

Please forgive my delay in replying to your request to join the Vector Toy Drive steering committee.

As we know, the annual toy drive is one of our company's most high-profile community activities. Cheering the hearts of disadvantaged children is its own reward. But the toy drive also reinforces the commitment of our brand to support those in need.

Your work in organizing the toy drive is commendable. I regret I cannot lend you a hand this year.

Please keep me in mind for the next season.

Regards,

Nick Bernheim
Business Unit Manager
Vector, Inc.
nickbernheim@vector.com

Tools

Praise the organization, event, or idea before issuing your refusal

A little bit of flattery goes a long way! When you compliment the readers on their activities and initiative, you communicate your respect for their efforts. Consequently, they're apt to be more understanding when you refuse to join in.

Use phrases such as "as we know" to indicate that you're on the same team

Expressions such as, "We are all concerned about…" and "We are each aware that…" emphasize that both reader and writer are part of the same collective. "We" draws attention to your similarities, not to your differences. By taking the time to slip in a "we" phrase in your e-mail, you reinforce your membership with the group.

Don't feel compelled to give a reason for a refusal

That old business saying, "Don't explain, don't apologize," might be a bit brisk, or even rude, in a period calling for greater business accountability and transparency. But that doesn't mean you must give detailed reasons for your refusal, either. When the explanation might appear predictable or defensive, such as, "I'm overwhelmed with work right now" or "My life is falling apart because of the divorce" it's better to avoid the excuse altogether. Your readers may speculate on your reasons, if they're so inclined. And who knows—they may come up with a more professionally viable explanation than the one you would have offered. As long as you affirm respect for current activities and interest in future projects, your lack of explanation is covered.

Keep the doors open by asking the reader to try again later

Assure the readers that you're not saying no forever. The next time around, you may have very specific reasons for accepting. Or you may need to make your own request of the readers one day. All the more reason to keep the door propped open.

$\mathcal{N}$etiquette

E-mail is one of the most effective ways of reinforcing positive interpersonal relationships. But using e-mail to reinforce human bonds is also one of the most difficult skills to learn. You can't shake hands with a computer and feel confidence in the grip.

Maintaining and building relationships through writing concerns every aspect of the writing process—from conception through layout.

—If a message is structured so that the main points appear in logical order, you show concern for the reader's comprehension.

—If you choose your vocabulary carefully—such as using "possibly" when you mean "possibly" and "probably" when you mean "probably"—you're writing a message that the reader can rely on.

—If you take the time to point out positive observations before your negative ones, the reader will be more receptive and understanding.

—If you layout the message so that the reader can easily read or even skim, then you're showing respect for the reader's time.

These—and many other—writing skills and techniques shore up losses incurred through standard use of an impersonal communication medium. In the old days, you would have met often with colleagues over lunch at the club. But when our business colleagues span the globe, when conflicting work schedules are endemic, and when the time it takes to meet someone face to face doesn't justify the outcome, e-mail is the main vehicle we have for fostering loyalty and building partnerships. And it works—provided the writing skills are up to speed.

Writing well pays off

The complexity of written communication allows us to focus on a specific feature. But because different aspects of language are related, improvement in one area often leads to improvement in other areas.

Apology for Inappropriate Behavior

Subject Announcement

Acknowledgment of Error

Assurance

Goodwill Close

Leslie,

This e-mail is difficult for me to write, because I realize that I have offended you.

Because my actions this morning could be interpreted as inappropriate, I wish to offer my sincere, heartfelt apologies.

You have my full personal assurance that an unpleasant incident such as this will never happen again.

I have always felt that we have a pleasant and productive work relationship. I respect and value your presence in the office. I truly hope that we can immediately put this upset behind us.

Sincerely,

Tom Clerk
Investment Analyst
Vector, Inc.
tomclerk@vector.com

Tools

Always apologize right away

No excuses, no procrastination—get it over with, ASAP. The longer you wait, the more reluctant your apology will appear. A delayed apology worsens the damage because it suggests that you didn't really want to apologize, or think you had to, in the first place. Which suggests you don't really mean your apology, either.

A prompt apology, however, sends the signal that your reader's feelings take precedence over other matters. If you show the reader that you want to right the wrong immediately, your reader is more likely to be forgiving.

Acknowledge what you did wrong

No need to go into a lot of detail! But you do need to refer to your offense—otherwise you look as if you're begrudging the apology, or that you're uncertain as to what, exactly, you did wrong. If you omit mentioning the event, you might even send the signal that you're in denial, which strongly suggests that you'll repeat the bad behavior in the future.

Owning up to bad behavior suggests that you're honest—and honesty has a very high value in Anglophone cultures. In other words, you may have had an error in judgment and misbehaved. But if you're honest about what you did wrong, then you're probably still a good egg, after all.

Assure the reader that you value your business relationship

You have to state outright that the reader is an important colleague. You can't assume that he or she "knows." Because you've offended the reader, the relationship is in doubt. The quickest way to get it back on track is to remind the reader that the relationship is important and that you're going to work to maintain it.

Be sincere

Sincerity is a tricky issue in writing—not because it's difficult to communicate, but because it's difficult to pin down. As with many writing issues, the sincerity of the text exists everywhere and nowhere. Think of a great car or a beautiful living room—it's hard to point out one definitive feature that makes it work, precisely because success doesn't usually reside in a single feature. It resides in the combination of parts united in a synergistic whole.

The same thing holds true for sincerity in writing. It's hard to point to one particular word, such as "sorry," and say that the e-mail is sincere or isn't sincere. A sincere e-mail can't be reduced to a single word. It has to do with the combination of words, the selection of the vocabulary, and the rhythm and pattern of the sentences. And yet sincerity comes across. Readers pick up on it fast. So the best thing to do is to write your apology honestly and sincerely. The odds are that the reader will sense sincerity, too.

Options

I wish to offer...   It is regrettable that I...

I regret...   It was wrong of me to...

I apologize...   It was an error in my judgment to...

I'm sorry...   I would like to excuse myself for...

I feel badly about...   Please allow me to apologize for...

I feel very awkward about...   Please accept my apologies for...

Communications gap

Most workers haven't been trained to write e-mail! But the jobs we have rely more on our e-mail communication skills than ever before. More than one generation of employees has been caught out by this! Workers land highly sought-after jobs only to discover that their written communication skills aren't up to par. Training in e-mail communication slipped through the cracks in the education system just at the moment when writing expertise became a requisite job skill.

Chapter Four

Vendors and Suppliers

Including

Confirming an Order

Call for Bids

Errors in Invoicing

Requesting Credit

Refusal of Credit

Change of Terms

$\mathcal{E}$dit

Before: reminder on an order

> YOUR WEBSITE MUST BE A REAL MESS BECAUSE I ORDERED SEVEN COLOR CARTRIDGES AT THE END OF LAST WEEK IN AN URGENT SITUATION AND THEY STILL HAVE NOT ARRIVED AT THE OFFICE ALTHOUGH THE ORDER CONFIRMATION CAME THROUGH A WHILE AGO AND THEY APPARENTLY CLEARED THE CREDIT CARD ON THE SAME DAY!!!!!! WHERE ARE THEY??????? WHAT IS REALLY HAPPENING?????? DON'T YOU GUYS FOLLOW THROUGH ON YOUR ORDERS RIGHT AWAY LIKE YOU SAY YOU DO ON YOUR WEBSITE OR IS THAT JUST BLAH-BLAH-BLAH. FWIW GET BACK TO ME ASAP BECAUSE IF YOU AREN'T ABLE TO GET THOSE CARTRIDGES TO US IMMEDIATELY I WILL FIND ANOTHER OFFICE SUPPLY COMPANY WHO IS JUST WAITING FOR THE BUSINESS AND WHO WILL DO WHAT THEY SAY WHEN THEY SAY IT. :-(

The problem

Layout! An all-caps text block is angry, furious, enraged. Capital letters shout, even scream. Worse yet, the anger and rage are reinforced by a single, forbidding mass of prose. Readers don't even have to read the e-mail to sense what's up. They know from a quick glance at the screen that insults and accusations are coming their way. Assaulting readers is not the most efficient way of winning them over to your side. In fact, it's a good way to ensure that you aren't taken seriously.

Tone! Accusations and threats usually don't further your cause. But they do inflict pain and make the reader angry. Threatening language—if you don't X, then I'll do Y—doesn't solve a problem. It often makes it worse.

Similarly, telling the reader that their business is "a REAL mess" sounds, at the very least, unprofessional and lacking in dignity. Facts have to be confronted—nasty, unruly feelings don't.

Sentence Structure! All-cap sentences that run on and on suggest that it's more than grammar that's out of control. Rather than helping you vent your anger, a furious, run-on sentence may have the opposite effect, drawing attention to and reinforcing negative, disproportionate feelings.

Juvenile Touches! Multiple explanation marks and question marks make you look like you've never understood how English punctuation works. Emoticons such as :-(reinforce the message that you're an underage professional or one who's never really matured in writing. The all-caps text and SMS abbreviations confirm the negative impression. Do you want the reader to take you seriously as a business professional?

The solution

Break up the text into paragraph units. Figure out the main facts you want to get across and group them according to the points you want to make. Get rid of the all-caps layout so that the reader isn't biased against you even before he or she reads in detail. You want your e-mail to be reader-friendly, otherwise it might not even be replied to.

Divide your feelings about the subject matter from the facts of the subject matter. When we're under the pressure of a deadline, it's not always easy to separate the wood from the flame. Edit out threats, accusations, and emotional words—the kinds of things you'd never say to a senior colleague whom you respect. If you can't say them to a colleague, you probably shouldn't say them to anyone else, either. Take a step back. Supply, instead, the facts that have fueled your emotions: what happened, when it happened, and what proof you have.

Control your sentences to control your thoughts and feelings. The quickest technique for curbing emotions is also one of the simplest: limit sentence length. Try to write in the shortest possible sentence units that you can. Grammatical restraint leads to restraint in other areas. You'll be surprised how clear and logical your points are when you can see them lined up as discreet, grammatical units.

Dump the juvenile effects. SMS acronyms, such as FWIW (for what it's worth), smileys, or emoticons work against professional business communication. Using words that belong on a cell phone or in a chat room suggest that you don't adhere to professional standards on the job. They may even suggest that you're emotionally stunted. Use them on your cell phone or in your personal correspondence, but don't let them sully your professional e-mail.

Although some acronyms, such as FYI and ASAP, have passed into dictionaries of standard English usage, most abbreviations don't make it across the threshold.

After: reminder on an order

Jim,

In the past I've done regular business with your site. I have not been disappointed with either FutureOffice products or services until last week.

On Monday, August 12, I ordered seven color cartridges (NLS 580) with two-day delivery. On August 13, I received confirmation on my order (#37-004-215). As of Monday, August 19, the cartridges have not been delivered.

Because I know you value our business, I know you'll rectify the situation immediately.

I look forward to hearing from you soon.

Regards,

Gloria Fromm, Assistant Director
Vector, Inc.
gloriafromm@vector.com

Tools

Use a normative mix of upper and lower case letters

English capitalization is designed to increase reader comprehension. Capitals are not simply decorative. They are meaning-*full*, not meaning-*less*. For example, when a capital occurs at the beginning of sentence, it announces a new idea. When a capital signals a proper noun, it's telling the reader that there's a specific detail he or she should pay attention to. A capital imparts a kind of grammatical respect. Capitalized words are arguably somehow more important than lowercase words—the difference, say, between "country" and "Australia."

Consequently, proper use of capital letters tells the reader that you know the code of normative English. It says that you're a professional who plays by the rules. You're someone who deserves attention and whose e-mail should be taken seriously. But when an e-mail is all caps or all lowercase, you're giving the impression that you're juvenile or lazy or both. It doesn't take that much brainpower to learn how to capitalize in English. Most kids figure it out.

Recognize that normative punctuation is more emphatic than excessive punctuation

Just as a loud scarf or tie can ruin an otherwise perfectly good professional look, too many punctuation marks can bring down the authority of an e-mail. One explanation point, used properly, carries more emphasis than 10 used improperly.

*I*nbox

When reading your email, you should consider the following points to evaluate which emails are successful and which ones aren't.

—Which e-mail is factual?

—Which one uses specific details to persuade?

—Which one reflects professional skill and status?

—Which one calls writing skills into question?

—Which e-mail is more likely to receive a quick, favorable reply?

Confirming an Order

Subject
Announcement

Changes in Order

Shipping

Goodwill
Close

Linsey,

I am writing to confirm the changes you made on January 4, 2007, to Vector Order # 12BG591 for 12 reams of Unbleached Recycled Paper.

We have added 6 reams of Safe Bleach Paper, and we will group the order together for shipping. We have also added 3 boxes of red roller pens, 1 box of number 2 pencils and 1 electric sharpener.

Because you indicated that you need the products as soon as possible, I have sent them by 3-day surface mail.

Considering that the holidays are over, I don't think there will be any hitches. Please let me know if there's anything else we can help you with.

Regards,

Bo Pwzekloz
Earth Papers, Inc
www.earthpapers.com

Tools

Don't be comma phobic!

Most business professionals still wing it when it comes to the comma. Why? Because commas seem complicated—too many rules, too many exceptions. Comma-phobic writers don't know that most business e-mail depends on a limited number of sentence patterns. So there's only a limited number of commas that you need to learn.

Opt for a comma after your reader's name in the salutation

Beware of automatic grammar checks! Some word processing programs try to pressure you into using a colon (:) after the salutation. The colon sets a formal tone appropriate in an official writing situation, say, in the context of legal documents. Most of the time, though, a comma will do.

Put a conventional comma between the day and the year, and after the year

It's "January 4, 2007," when the date appears in full. But if it's just "January 2007," no comma is required between the month and the year.

Don't forget one of the most common commas

FANBOYS is an acronym for the following conjunctions: For, And, Nor, But, Or, Yet, So. You use a comma between two complete sentences joined by a FANBOYS conjunction.

(Sentence), for *(sentence)*.
        , and
        , nor
        , but
        , or
        , yet
        , so

For example, a FANBOYS comma appears in the following sentence: "We have added 6 reams of Safe Bleach Paper, and we will group the order together for shipping."

Use a comma to divvy up (almost all) components in a list

In the example, "We have also added 3 boxes of red roller pens, 1 box of pencils and 1 electric sharpener," the comma goes between the roller pens and the box of pencils. Depending on the style of your company, you don't have to put one in front of the "and 1 electric sharpener." That comma is called a serial comma, and usually comes into play when there's potential confusion. In the following sentence, "We have also added 3 boxes of red roller pens, 1 box of number 2 pencils, and black and white tape," you need a comma before the tape so that the "and" between components in the list isn't confused with the "and" between adjectives.

Gently mark the boundary between the introductory clause and the main clause with a comma

Often the introductory clause begins with one of the following words— "although," "because," "since," "when," or "if." For example, "Since you indicated that you need the products as soon as possible, I have sent them by 3-day surface mail."

The introductory clause might also begin with an "ing" word, as it does in the following example, "Considering that the holidays are over, I don't think there will be any hitches."

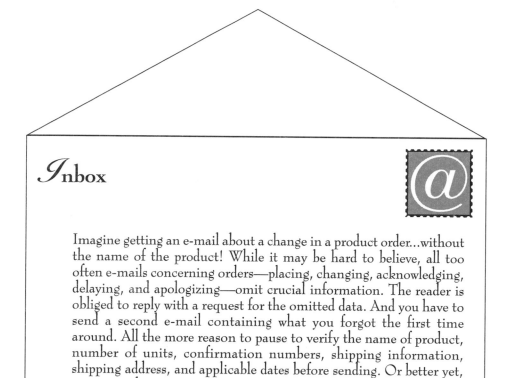

Inbox

Imagine getting an e-mail about a change in a product order...without the name of the product! While it may be hard to believe, all too often e-mails concerning orders—placing, changing, acknowledging, delaying, and apologizing—omit crucial information. The reader is obliged to reply with a request for the omitted data. And you have to send a second e-mail containing what you forgot the first time around. All the more reason to pause to verify the name of product, number of units, confirmation numbers, shipping information, shipping address, and applicable dates before sending. Or better yet, use a template.

Netiquette

Business e-mail follows hardcopy rules for capitals. Although you may be tempted to use all lowercase for the laidback and cool look, it isn't going to help you get ahead in the business world. And the all-caps option makes you look angry or hysterical.

Proper usage of capitals has the opposite effect—you reinforce your written communication skills. The right mix of capitals and lower case sends the message to reader that you know the code—the code of correctly written English. And you do. It's reinforced every time you read the newspapers, a book, or an edited Website. You may not be able to control every nuance of the language when you write, but you process correct grammatical signals every time you read quality prose. The knowledge is there—you just have to make it conscious.

Capitalization has to do with authority—more important and specific things, use capitals, while the run-of-the-mill noun is left with lower case. Capitalization is a way of paying respect, in writing, to the power of a thing's existence.

Consider, for example, the difference between "Through-Screen Security Camera" and "Through-screen security camera" (or even "through-screen security camera"). Which one is the most official? The most authoritative? Which camera looks as if it'll work better? Which one is the most reliable? Which one would you rather buy?

Capitals do more than simply garner respect and manifest authority. Capitalizing also gives the skim-prone business reader essential comprehension clues. Before the brain even gets to the finer activities of word identification, the capitals have already had an impact. The capitals tell us that we're receiving specific information before we even know what it is.

Use capitals for proper nouns—names of people, products, documents, and places. When in doubt about whether to capitalize, look it up in other documents, such as prior e-mails, booklets, labels, and Websites.

Call for Bids

Anselm,

Subject
Announcement
Vector, Inc. is seeking bids for redecoration of the Executive Sales Offices in Hawthorne, New Jersey.

Requirements
This redecoration includes:

- 5 shared offices
- 7 private offices
- 1 executive office
- 1 executive office reception area
- 1 small meeting room
- 1 conference room
- 1 main reception area
- 1 staff room

Constraint 1
Because the company is in full global expansion, we want our business interior to reflect our global outlook in both color and materials. The message we want to send is: international.

Constraint 2
We also want to send a strong ecological message. Please note: We will not accept products that are in anyway associated with environmental hazards in the production, manufacturing or maintenance of materials.

Deadline
The deadline for bids is June 12, 2007. Detailed specifications are attached.

Goodwill
Close
Feel free to contact me if you need more information.

Regards,

Jayne Holmes
Human Resources Support
Vector, Inc.
jayneholmes@vector.com

Tools

Recognize the colon as an e-mail ally

Those two dots, arranged vertically one on top of the other, are a quick and snappy way to make a point. The colon is an important partner in e-mail because it lends itself to concision and speed.

Use a dutiful colon before a long list

Introduce the list, follow it by the colon, then catalogue each of the elements. For example, "This redecoration includes: 5 shared offices, 7 private offices, 1 executive office, 1 executive reception area, 1 small meeting room, 1 conference room, 1 main reception area, 1 stock room, and 1 staff room."

Call upon the colon to dramatize a key word or phrase at the end of a sentence

This usage of the colon is a little like whisking away a velvet cloth to reveal the prize. You can almost hear the drum roll…or at least an emphatic "taa-daa!" You pause when you encounter this colon—a small pause, to be sure—but it's enough to draw attention to the words that follow. For example, "The message we want to send is: international."

Use a colon like a bugle call at the beginning of a sentence

This colon does double-duty by introducing a point and insisting that the reader focus on it. That's why you're familiar with the usage in the previous e-mail, "Please note: We will not accept materials that are in anyway associated with environmental hazards."

But the please-note colon is just one among many. E-mail has spawned a range of variations that are quick, effective, and stylish.

Look: I would like to discuss this further…

Consider the problem: Vector has exceeded targets in sales, but…

Stop: This line of action will only complicate the situation…

Wait: Let's hold off on this decision until…

OK: Let's reconsider our position in the next draft…

Here's why: The meeting resulted in a new strategic marketing campaign…

That's true: We are in a period of belt-tightening…

No way: You've misunderstood their intentions…

$\mathcal{O}$ptions

Feel free to contact me if you need more information...

I'd be happy to supply additional information...

If you'd like to discuss the project in detail, please phone me at...

If you need more information, please contact me at...

Please get back to me for more information...

Please don't hesitate to contact me regarding this project...

Please give me a call and we can discuss the details.

Please let me know if I can provide more information.

Please contact me with any questions you might have.

Imitation is not plagiarism

Plagiarism is a serious offense that involves taking someone else's ideas or works and passing them off as your own, usually for financial gain. For plagiarism to occur, one author has ownership over intellectual property that another author takes without payment or acknowledgment.

If you took a well-written note of congratulations to the team for good results and copied it, erased the author's name and put your own in its place, you would be plagiarizing. If you took the same note and used it as a guideline, changing the wording and organization to suit your context and purpose, you are not plagiarizing. You are imitating.

Errors in Invoicing

Subject
Announcement

Joyce,

Yesterday, May 15, I received the April e-invoice from Interior Green (please see attached). This invoice is incorrect.

Situation

As I discussed yesterday with your associate, Braunwyn Michaels, Interior Green is no longer caring for the balcony gardens in the Vector executive offices. We have replaced annuals with succulents that do not require regular gardening maintenance. Vector notified Interior Green regarding the termination of the service contract on March 23 (see note below). We will, however, continue to use your services for the entry garden and atrium.

Rectification

Please revise the billing statement by removing one month of balcony maintenance and send me a cancelled invoice.

Goodwill
Close

Thank you for your prompt attention to this matter.

Regards,

Richard Strelling
Accounts Payable
Vector, Inc.
richardstrelling@vector.com

*T*ools

Use "please," but use it sparingly

"Please," properly used, sets an elegant tone. It shows respect for the reader. It suggests that the writer is deserving of respect, too. Courtesy usually receives positive attention, in business as in other aspects of life. We're not cretins, after all.

Remember that "please" has ladder-climbing value

"Please" sends the signal that the writer is not only polite, but also has class. And the higher you climb the career ladder, the more important social graces become.

Upper-level managers want to be surrounded by people similar to them. If you aspire to their ranks, follow their cues. And not just in business. Look at how they dress, eat, speak, what they do on *their* time off, and especially how they write their official, employee-wide e-mails.

Well-brought-up folks who are sure of themselves are polite most of the time; those who unsure of their performance either overdo the politeness and grovel, or omit it altogether. Using "please" properly enhances your authority.

But don't overdo the "please"

Too many "pleases" in a short e-mail can make you look obsequious. You want to send a strong, confident message, not a submissive one. One too many pleases, and you end up begging.

Use an artfully placed "please" to take the edge off imperatives

A well-placed "please" at the beginning of an e-mail will resonate in all the right places.

For example, use "please" for the first imperative ("please see the attached e-invoice") and drop it for subsequent mentions ("see note below").

Use a "thank you" to oblige action

"Thank you" can be used to ignal sincere gratefulness, or it can be used to oblige action. Most people usually like to be thanked for something that they've done. If you thank the reader in advance for something you want him or her to do, the odds go up that they'll actually do it. Or at least they'll think twice before they don't!

Netiquette

Be careful with attachments! Let's face it: Many attachments in the business world are optional. Some you have to open, because your job depends on it. Others you can open when you have time. And some you just delete.

In order to encourage the reader to open the attachment—and maybe even print it and read it—you have to introduce it properly. You don't want the reader to treat the attachment as if it were intruding on the e-mail, as though it were a crass, uninvited guest.

The standard introductory methods are the ones you already know. You either refer to the attachment in the body of the e-mail, as in "The attachment shows the latest figures," or you follow a statement in the body of the e-mail with a parenthetical (Please see attached.) Use a parenthetical (see attached) or (attached) with every subsequent attachment.

Attachment announcements go at the ends of things—the end of a sentence, the end of a paragraph, the end of an e-mail. If you tell the reader to look for an attachment in the middle of a sentence, it's a little like getting a phone call in the middle of a movie. It jars. It interrupts. It interferes with the delivery of ideas.

Worse yet, many business writers also make the mistake of repeating information, verbatim, from the attachment in the accompanying e-mail. You don't want to repeat ideas that are already laid out in the attachment; you want to summarize the general ideas contained in an attachment in your own words. Otherwise, why would you bother attaching the document in the first place?

An attachment doesn't compete with the e-mail. An attachment doesn't overtake the e-mail. An attachment complements the e-mail.

> **E-mail speeds writing up**
> **when we may need to slow it down**
>
> High-speed connectivity encourages us to speed outselves up, too. But we should fight the urge to accelerate our tasks when it comes to e-mail. Taking the time to carefully write an e-mail usually leads to efficiency, while rapidly banging out an e-mail usually leads to errors that we don't see, let alone correct.

Requesting Credit

Subject
Announcement

Justification 1

Justification 2

Value-Added
Incentive

Goodwill
Close

Cris,

As you know, Vector, Inc. is restructuring to mutually benefit our longstanding business relationships with Lumina Corp. For the same reason, Vector requires credit extension.

Vector's reconciliated accounts present a strong case for extending the line to 50K. While in the short term, the debt ratio will temporarily increase, so will the margins.

By May 2008, our debt-to-equity ratio will reflect gains from joint marketing agreements as well as amendments in factors of production. The extended line allows Vector to capitalize on opportunities while reducing accrued expenses. The full financial statement is attached.

As Vector expands existing operations in Central and South America, it will open new markets for Lumina Corp. I look forward to discussing the details of these incentives over the phone prior to our meeting. Please e-mail me your availability.

I am always available to provide additional information.

Regards,

Ambra Greason
Senior Accounts Analyst
Vector Dimensional
ambragreason@vector.com

Tools

Stay cool and confident, even when the request is large and unlikely

Writing has a funny way of communicating truth. You can read an e-mail and know that the reader is sincere, or read a different e-mail and have a clear idea that the writer is bluffing. Often it's difficult, if not impossible, to point to exact words, phrases, or ideas in which truthfulness resides.

The reason is that truthfulness doesn't always anchor at specific points in the written language. It often emerges at a higher level of organization, in the holistic network of communication implicit throughout the document. Truth values, in other words, are often the product of synthesis, not analysis.

You want to adopt your best business persona when you write your e-mail, particularly the difficult e-mails. If you write the e-mail under duress, a sensitive reader will get the vibe. Or if you write with a clear idea that your request will meet with doom, it probably will.

Use facts to convince the reader

Because business is deeply committed to rationalism—logic, objectivity, and empirical data—a well-constructed argument is your best ammunition. Lay out the facts logically, one by one. Use the sequence of facts to garner momentum. Add extra incentive at the end. Use crisp and clear sentences, and keep emotions at bay. Then, regardless of the outcome, you know you've done the best job you possibly can.

Netiquette

E-mail favors simple tenses. Because business e-mail is pragmatic (information is communicated from the writer to the reader with a specific purpose in mind) many fancy hardcopy features, such as those rarified embellishments and sublime literary affects, get sidelined. For example, complicated verb tenses with foreboding names, such as "past perfect passive progressive" aren't often required in a deal narrative or contract update.

In business e-mail, the rule of thumb is: Use the simplest tense possible. Why? Because many writers needlessly complicate their sentences by choosing the wrong tense. Writers who are unsure of their writing style or who speak multiple languages most often make this mistake.

"Vector is being restructured," "Vector has restructured," "Vector has been restructured," "Vector will be restructured," "Vector will be restructuring," "Vector will have been restructuring," "Vector will be being restructured," "Vector will have had restructuring," all express different meanings that may be handy in a specific context. But most of the time in business e-mail, complicated verb tenses just add clutter.

The three most useful present tenses in business e-mail are: 1) the simple present "Vector requires a credit extension"; 2) the simple present progressive "Vector is restructuring" (present to-be verb + -ing participle); and 3) present modals "Vector will open markets." These tenses can do most of the work of the other present-tense verbs in English. Don't use one of the other tenses unless you know you have to.

Similarly, the simple past tense is usually favored. "Vector restructured" communicates more efficiently than "Vector has had restructuring." And "Vector required credit" communicates more actively and concisely than "Vector had been requiring credit."

Just by using a simple, direct, straightforward verb tense in the past or present, you can write with greater ease and elegance. Your sentences will be lighter, quicker, and more active. As an added bonus, you'll look more confident, too.

Do...

Banish all unconscious repetition in your e-mails—repetition usually means you're not sure you've made your point. It suggests a lack of confidence.

Use amplifiers sparingly. "It was an important concession" is usually more effective than "it was a very important concession" or even a "very, very important concession."

Go easy on superlatives, e.g., "one of the most interesting outcomes" is more effective than "the most interesting outcome." Going to extremes often raises doubts.

Don't...

Make the mistake of returning to a point for the reader's benefit—in a short e-mail, it's often unnecessary and risks insulting the reader.

Succumb to words such as "really," "so," "very," and so on, whenever you can. These words are used for emotional intensity that is usually out of place in the business world.

Refusal of Credit

Subject Announcement

List of Conditions

Refusal

Goodwill Close

Mick,

Thank you for your e-mail of Sept. 21, requesting an extension of Vector's credit line. The request for 50K is likely to be approved in the future, provided:

- variance figures meet threshold requirements of 7M
- products and operations diverge shared lines
- weighed capital is at 10 percent of the 15M marker

As present, the financial report is far from transparent. Lumina cannot accept greater exposure without a better idea of what we're dealing with.

Please give me a call if you want to discuss this further.

Regards,

Allen Touquas
Senior Credit Analyst
Lumina Corp.
allentouquas@luminacorp.com

*T*ools

Leave the door open

Because business is built on relationships, you want to work to maintain lines of communication rather than pulling them down. You never know when you and your reader will cross paths again.

If the tables are turned next time around, what do you want the reader to remember about how you do business? That you're clear, direct, and respectful? Or brusque and dismissive?

Keep the door open by stating refusals in positive terms. Even negative news, when it's presented properly, loses its edge. Business insiders know that what at first might look like a defeat is, in fact, an opportunity.

Give the reader specific conditions to fulfill

Refusals, similar to acceptances, usually aren't definitive—they're conditional. If business factors change, so does the credit. So instead of saying "this wasn't good enough" and "that wasn't right," provide the reader with exact requirements to meet in order to attain objectives. When you give the reader something to aim for, the ball is back in his or her court.

Put the conditions in a list

One of the cleverest of ways of drawing attention to information is also one of the simplest: put it in a list, set off from the surrounding paragraphs. The added white space provides focus, and the introductory colon adds a dash of formality. The result is that the information catches the eye in a different way.

When information is presented differently, it's understood differently, too. In other words, a list buried inside a large text block and a list set off in the middle of the page aren't the same list, though they may contain identical content. A list embedded in a text block blurs into the surrounding information, negating its own importance; a list set off from the text block insists on its own significance and instantly attracts the reader's attention.

Try dropping numerical markers

Using a dash (—) or a bullet point (•) to head off your list makes the page appear less heavy and cluttered than the numerical system of 1, 2, and 3. Numerical markers aren't neutral; dashes and bullet points are.

Numbers suggest a hierarchy of information, often ranked in the order of importance. 1 is more important than 5, and 5 is more important than 17. Because numerical markers have meaning, they require a few nano-seconds of cognition to evaluate.

A series of dashes or bullet points doesn't necessarily differ from one to the next. The fourth bullet point in a list is pretty much the same as the first bullet point. The reader doesn't have to determine the difference in rank, as he or she might when 1 and 4 are being used.

Symbols send the signal that the items aren't necessarily in a sequential order. Just as importantly, symbols lighten up the page by reducing the amount of information sent to the reader. Just make sure that you choose normative symbols, not weird ones. Listing items with a ✎ or a ✿ looks cutesy. Business e-mail is not cutesy.

Netiquette

Numbers in e-mail are usually less fussy than numbers in hardcopy. In many e-mail contexts, it's not necessary to write out fifteen when 15 will do, just as $200 is more likely than $200.00 (and certainly more likely than two-hundred U.S. dollars).

In business e-mail, where sums shoot through cyberspace with dazzling speed, no one has time for $75,000.00 when $75K will do. And no one really wants to see 800,000,000,000 when 800B will do the job.

Standard abbreviations include: K for thousands, M for millions, B for billions, and T for trillions. Monetary units, such as dollars and pounds, are often abbreviated with the currency symbol. When competing currencies threaten confusion, use international monetary abbreviations, such as EP for Egyptian pounds, or AD for Australian dollars.

Hardcopy options for expressing numbers, such as fifty-five billion United States of America dollars, find application in official documents and in formal, contractual contexts. But when you're bouncing e-mails around the firm, or from one business partner to the next, efficiency of the communication takes precedence over tradition.

Change of Terms

Subject Announcement

Bad News

Good News

Goodwill Close

Sonya,

As I mentioned today, July 13, on the phone, Vector, Inc. is committed to maintaining our business relationship with Lumina. Mutual profitability is the reason behind our request to amend our supply contracts as soon as possible.

In a climate of financial austerity, Vector, Inc. is reducing costs by restricting new equipment purchases. Similarly, aggressive debt restructuring has led to a tighter balance sheet in which outlays are subject to close scrutiny. Moreover, losses in the Q3 supply sector have hit hard. Consequently, we cannot maintain our current quotas from Lumina.

But we do not want to damage our long-term partnership. Nor do we want injure the network we've worked so hard together to build. To offset the short-term quota reduction, Vector proposes extending the service agreements over a 3-year term.

I have attached a draft of the paperwork here for your consideration. Please get back to me with any questions or comments you might have.

Regards,

Yon Howard
Senior Business Unit Manager
Vector, Inc.
yonhoward@vector.com

Tools

Use cause-and-effect to make your case

English is hardwired for cause-and-effect. Consider, for example, the subject/verb/complement structure of many English language sentences—it's almost as if the energy in the noun is routed via the verb to the destination in the complement. In "Vector buys Lumina subsidiary," the energy represented by Vector acts on the target (or in this case, "buys Lumina subsidiary").

In other words, English syntax (word order) has its own logic. Or to put it another way, you could even say that English is hardwired to suit some forms of expression over others.

When you use the forms hardwired into a language, you take a well-worn path. The odds of losing your way diminish, while veering through unmarked terrain usually leads to problems. Writing in forms that go against hardwiring can be challenging, as anyone who has tried to import standard means of expression from one language into the next knows only too well.

So when you foreground cause-and-effect in your writing, you've got the weight and authority of the language behind you. Lucky you!

Figure out how one thing leads to another

In order to make a successful cause-and-effect argument, you have to put your points in the right order. One thing leads to another thing, or maybe a pair of things. Then those things lead to a result. When you put the causes in the right order, the result usually has an air of inevitability. That's why when readers confront a tight cause-and-effect argument, they're often tempted to agree. Or at the very least, they have to look harder for reasons not to.

Use cause-and-effect linking words to build your argument

Sequential linking words give your cause-and-effect argument logical force by highlighting the relationship between the elements. The words "To begin with," "Next," "In addition," and "Therefore" carry meaning, even before the rest of the sentence is filled in. These and other linking words supply structure and logic. If they preface convincing points, the odds are in your favor that you're creating a strong case that will be difficult to dispute.

*A*dvice

Less is more, but is it enough?

Business writers suffering from CYA (Cover Your Ass) syndrome are usually not effective communicators. Why? Because in the words of one CEO I spoke with, CYA sufferers "detail every issue to death." In other words, they make their point, but because they're afraid of being called down for omitting crucial information, they include far too much. For fear of leaving something out, every single thing goes in. An e-mail that could have been three slick paragraphs expands into an unwieldy two-pager (with attachments).

These writers forget that readers don't *have* to know everything. In fact, most of the time readers don't *want* to know everything. The higher up the readers are on the management ladder, the bigger the picture they have. For example, if you're alerting your boss to a glitch in manufacturing that will impact inventory with significant delivery delays, the circumstances regarding how you learned about the problem probably won't be important. The reader needs enough information to take action, not enough to replicate your experience, your analysis, or your assessment.

Ironically, an onslaught of information usually doesn't achieve the desired effect. Readers are less likely to be convinced by voluminous prose than they are by a few, well-chosen sentences. Mass does not equal might. Extra information distracts readers from the main idea in the e-mail—provided that you have, of course, *identified* the main idea. If you're digressing a lot, you probably lost sight of it. An e-mail overcharged with information easily collapses under its own weight.

Worse yet, redundancy and repetition undercut veracity. If you write it once, we believe you. Write it again and again, and we don't. For example, if you keep going on about how hard your team worked, how many hours they put in, how they kept the midnight oil burning, how they sacrificed their personal lives for the project, you might raise the specter of exaggeration. And why would you exaggerate? Probably because you didn't work hard enough in the first place. The line between insistence and defensiveness is easily drawn, as Lady MacBeth knows only too well.

Most of the top business professionals I've met don't waste words. They're too busy. They say what they have to say, or write what they have to write, and get on with the next task. If a CEO says someone has done a good job, it's enough.

For all these reasons, saying less is usually more effective than saying more...provided there's enough! Summarizing the outcome of a meeting in a short paragraph is usually effective, but a one-sentence summary isn't (and neither is a detailed play-by-play). So how do you know when enough is enough?

The answer depends, in part, on what kind of paragraph or e-mail you're building. Are you making an assertion? You need one or two examples. Are you explaining a process? Make sure you have all the steps. Are you providing logistical information? Then the who, what, where, when, why should be covered. Are you making a request? Better give two or three reasons why. Or are you constructing a cause-and-effect argument? Then make sure you've included all the main links between ideas.

Writers who have difficulty supplying enough information usually just need to be more specific. Instead of writing, "We need to cut costs," it's more effective to back up the assertion with reasons. "We need to cut costs because Q1 losses in bio-pharmaceuticals have led to a 12 percent shortfall in revenues."

But don't go overboard! The same idea, riddled with details, sinks: "We need to really think about and consider our cost-cutting strategies in view of the fact that substantial Q1 losses in the plant protein products in bio-pharmaceuticals, particularly those manufactured in Holland by our subsidiary, and to a lesser degree, those manufactured by our BP in France, have negatively impacted our profits so that we have had the unforeseen result of a 12 percent shortfall in our yearly revenues."

In my experience, writers who don't say enough are in the minority—most of the time, it's the other way around. How little or how much information you need to include depends as much on the reader as it does on the writer. Look at it this way: You know what point your e-mail needs to make. You've been hired, in part, because you can make that point. Don't send the message that you're not confident either in your writing style or in your position by overdoing it or under-doing it.

Forget what you learned in class

Writing effective e-mails at work does not require soul-searching, elaborate pre-writing, peer editing, long talks with mentors, or keeping a log of the writing process. Business e-mail is product-oriented, not process-oriented.

CHAPTER FIVE

Sales and Marketing

INCLUDING

Invitation to an Open House

Announcing a New Sales Rep

Pitch for Appointment

Employee Discounts

Targeted Product Launch

Launch Announcement

Marketing Query

Invitation to an Open House

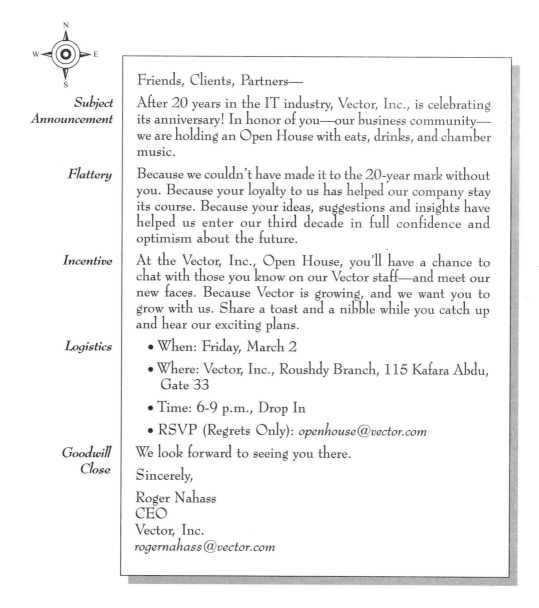

Friends, Clients, Partners—

Subject Announcement

After 20 years in the IT industry, Vector, Inc., is celebrating its anniversary! In honor of you—our business community—we are holding an Open House with eats, drinks, and chamber music.

Flattery

Because we couldn't have made it to the 20-year mark without you. Because your loyalty to us has helped our company stay its course. Because your ideas, suggestions and insights have helped us enter our third decade in full confidence and optimism about the future.

Incentive

At the Vector, Inc., Open House, you'll have a chance to chat with those you know on our Vector staff—and meet our new faces. Because Vector is growing, and we want you to grow with us. Share a toast and a nibble while you catch up and hear our exciting plans.

Logistics

- When: Friday, March 2
- Where: Vector, Inc., Roushdy Branch, 115 Kafara Abdu, Gate 33
- Time: 6-9 p.m., Drop In
- RSVP (Regrets Only): *openhouse@vector.com*

Goodwill Close

We look forward to seeing you there.

Sincerely,

Roger Nahass
CEO
Vector, Inc.
rogernahass@vector.com

Tools

Use emotion to get the reader's attention

Exclamation points, emotional language, a chummy tone—these are the hallmarks of sales. The best way to attract readers is through emotion. Once you've got their attention, then you can follow through. But get their attention first, otherwise you may be wasting your time.

Use conscious repetition to persuade the reader

Even when it's read silently, language is still sound. The reader "hears" the words in his or her head. You can take advantage of the aural dimension through repetition, which creates a rhythmic effect through repeated components. Repetition appeals to the reader's emotions and, consequently, captures their attention. But be careful! Too much repetition (especially *unconscious* repetition) quickly results in boredom.

Use flattery as a persuasive tool

Some people think of flattery as a kind of falsehood. Not so! Flattery is an ideal observation made in an ideal world. In other words, it has to do with forgetting the downside and spotlighting the upside. It derives force from sincerity, not from mendacity. Optimism is key.

Netiquette

When sending a bulk e-mail, try to humanize the salutation. Because e-mail lets us reach hundreds if not thousands of correspondents with a push of a button, the technology itself undercuts personalization.

Use friendly, nongendered words, such as "Friends" or "Colleagues," that describe your real or potential relationship to the readers. Avoid dull, old-country phrases, such as "Gentleman," or "Dear Sir or Madame." These kinds of openings make you look uptight and outdated, when it's probably to your advantage to appear dynamic and forward thinking.

Similarly, "To Whom It May Concern" seems to still function in e-mail, though its use appears to be on the decline. The preference in bulk mail is for the neutral and sober salutation, "All." Some business writers soften the impersonality of this salutation by adding "Dear," as in "Dear All." You can also use "Dear Team," "Dear Crew," "Dear Coworkers," and so on to similar effect.

Announcing a New Sales Rep

Subject
Announcement

Drew,

I've enjoyed working together with you on Lumina Corp. accounts over the last year. Our business relationship has not only been mutually beneficial, but also transparent and reliable. That's why I feel certain you will pleased to be working with Gustaf Sorin.

Profile

Gustaf is taking over my position in the Vector sales department as Associate Sales Manager of the Poetics account. Formerly a Consultant at Duncan & Doolittle, Gustaf was a valuable member of the Marketing Task Force for the full range of Vector's Poetics SW. His ready grasp of the specifications, performance and potential of the Poetics systems caught Vector's eye. And it's no wonder, because Gustaf has an impressive background in systems programming.

Expectations

I feel certain that Gustaf will thoughtfully address your concerns about Poetics SW with the same honesty and knowledge that you've come to expect from Vector. He will be in touch with you in the coming days about the imprint issues we discussed last month.

Goodwill
Close

Please get back to me if there's any information that I can supply.

Regards,

Ellie Ezran
Manager, Poetics Software Sales and Representation
Vector Inc.
ellieezran@vector.com

Tools

Don't be naïve when it comes to explanation

Explanation is a standard writing strategy—so standard, in fact, that we take it for granted. Everybody can explain why an employee is a good performer or what the new packaging looks like, can't they?

Wrong. Explanation, as with every other writing strategy, involves specific techniques in order to arrive at a specific outcome. Explanation combines description, narration, exemplification, and analysis, among other writing techniques. But many writers assume they can easily explain something without really paying attention to what they're doing. And it shows.

Arrange sentences in a present-to-past pattern to explain "why"

When a promotion is announced, the question on everyone's mind is "why did so-and-so get the position?" The present-to-past setup emphasizes the facts behind a current development and makes the outcome appear to be a logical conclusion.

Describe so-and-so's background and qualifications, beginning with the *current* moment. Every other sentence in the paragraph should support the sentence that precedes it. No wonder so-and-so is the new sales rep! His or her last position was W, where he or she accomplished X. And before that, Y. And before that, Z. Present-to-past explanations emphasize results. The last thing that happened is more important than how we got there.

Arrange sentences in a past-to-present pattern to explain "how"

The *how* accentuates the play-by-play process, with one step leading to another leading to another and so on. Chronology lists the sequential steps in a process, while cause-and-effect accentuates the links between each step in the sequence. One simply lays down brick after brick; the other pays careful attention to the mortar.

Because they get to the end of the process by slightly different means, chronology and cause-and-effect present different results. Although both make the process clear, chronology is more neutral. The interpretation of the process is up the reader. Cause-and-effect steers the reader into thinking the process is inevitable, not happenstance.

Arrange sentences according to spatial logic to describe a tangible "what"

There are two main methods for describing an object or a place. The zoom technique either begins with the panorama and zooms in on a detail or vice versa. For example, if you want to describe an organic cereal box, you could start with the dimensions of the recycled paper box and end up with the bulging cheeks of the chewing child pictured on the front inset below the logos. Or vice versa.

The second technique for description involves framing the area by moving clockwise, counterclockwise, or in a grid around a visual object. For example, if you need to describe the partitioning of a Webpage, you could begin with the top banner, move to the left column, the right column, and the center column.

No matter which method you choose, the description should have some sort of spatial logic to it.

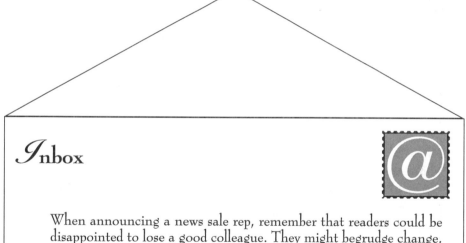

𝓘nbox

When announcing a news sale rep, remember that readers could be disappointed to lose a good colleague. They might begrudge change, or even feel resentful toward the new hire. They might even be worried that the subtle points in an agreement won't be honored. All the more reason to make sure your readers know they're getting the same attention that they've grown to rely on.

Reassure the reader by explaining why the new hire is perfect. Your sales accounts will be relieved by solid credentials, by having insight into the new hire, and by knowing that they will continue to receive the same consideration that they've come to expect.

Pitch for Appointment

Subject
Announcement

Freebie

Offer

Goodwill
Close

Xi,

I was among the many fans at your presentation last week, "Wired for Green," at the Vector, Inc. annual IT Conference. Given how accomplished you are in person, I was surprised to see how ineffective the copy is in your "Wired for Green" brochure.

I've taken the liberty of attaching a new version of the "Wired for Green" brochure—not because I want to point out the weaknesses of the original, but because I want to show you how much better the brochure can be. Ideas as impressive as yours require impressive prose, too. They need to be written as carefully as they were developed. And they should compliment your powerful visuals with the same level of intensity and rigor.

As a freelance copywriter with a background in social psychology, I specialize in using words to elicit specific responses in readers. My clients include several Fortune 500 groups. I am particularly drawn to your work because you bring to the business world an intuition for trends that is rare and vital. I believe I could help you improve your promotional tools and written communication style.

I am eager to know what you think of the attached version of "Wired for Green." I'll give your office a call this week to see if we can find a time to meet.

Regards,

Sydney Wiser
www.sydneywiser.com

$\mathcal{T}$ools

Always remind the prospect that you know them well

Contacting a prospect involves convincing him or her that there's a reason to pursue discussion. Try including specific information about the prospect's business and accomplishments. Sending the signal that you've done your homework also sends the signal that you won't waste time.

Offer a quick criticism of the reader's business

The idea here is not to emphasize where the business has gone wrong, but to focus on where the business can grow. Readers are usually intrigued by unexpected criticism, particularly if it's constructive. You want to package your criticism in such a way that it's an opportunity, not a liability. Use a direct, factual tone and stick to general observations. Too many details and you'll look like you're nagging. And we all know, naggers are more likely to ignored than heard.

Give the reader something for free

Nothing is more convincing than evidence! Telling the readers that you've done your homework, that you have the right product or service for them, and that they can see it for themselves is powerful bait, indeed. There's no reason to turn your offer down—or at least, they'll have to work hard to find one.

If the readers accept the freebie—or even *think* about accepting the freebie—they owe you something in return. It's the old I-do-something-for-you, and, you'll-do-something-for-me routine. Most folks don't grab and run. They feel obliged to thank you, and perhaps offer to do you a good turn.

Summarize credentials

Prospects appreciate references, whether those references are other clients with whom you've worked, testimonials from total strangers, or even statistical data from impersonal agencies. References present an illusion of objectivity that is often persuasive. It's easy to say, "I don't need your product," if you're facing the offer alone. It's more difficult to say "I don't need your product," if consumers you respect use it or if hoards of others say it's just the thing you need to make your life happier and more productive.

Make your pitch as a next-step proposition

Asking for too much undercuts your creditability. Professionals know that business proceeds incrementally, step by step. Your pitch should be intriguing enough to get an appointment. The interview is where you push for the contract or make the sale. If you try to do too much in a single e-mail, you give the game away.

Your job is to seduce the prospect, not to manipulate him or her. Whet their curiosity, get their attention, and appeal to their self-interest. But do it gently, almost playfully. Pressuring a prospect, particularly in the early stages of a sale, usually only results in nixing your chances.

Include a precise plan of action

Give the reader some wiggle room, but not too much. Indicate that you'll give him or her a call or send a follow-up e-mail in the coming days. And make certain you do what you say you're going to do! Establishing your reliability is tantamount to establishing professionalism. Even if your pitch doesn't result in an immediate sale, it may lead to a referral or a sale further down the line.

*O*ptions

I'll call you soon...

I'll give your office a call this week...

I'll be in touch in the coming days...

I'll follow up this e-mail with a phone call...

I'll contact your office this week for an appointment...

I'll send you an e-mail later on in the week to see if...

Employee Discounts

Dear Human Resources Manager,

*Subject
Announcement*

As manager of Go Organic, I would like to extend a 10% discount on Gourmet Lunchboxes to all full-time Vector, Inc. employees. The offer is good through end-2007.

*Product
Summary*

Go Organic specializes in light, gourmet meals prepared in our kitchens using products from Grow Organic farms. All our foodstuffs—fruits, vegetables, nuts and grains—are grown in biodynamic fields free of artificial pesticides and herbicides. Our livestock roam in fenced-in terrain, nourished on traditional feeds. Grow Organic oils and wines are of the highest qualities, renown as much for their taste as for their nutrients.

*Product
Profile*

Each Gourmet Lunchbox features a main-course salad accompanied by grain or bread, with a raw or prepared fruit dessert. Vegetarians might prefer the lemon-squash salad with basil quinoa and sautéed bananas, while others might choose the roasted chicken accompanied with walnut and spinach salad, with cornbread and fresh berries.

*Product
Range*

With 14 Go Organic Lunchboxes to choose from, there's an organic gourmet combination to suit every palette. We also have a full range of sandwiches, snacks and juices, each made on-site with our own Grow Organic ingredients.

To receive a 10%E discount, Vector, Inc. employees must present a current employee ID. We are open 24 hours—and of course, we deliver. If you have any questions on our offer, feel free to contact me at Go Organic, Wilson branch: 716-235-9897. Or visit our Website at *www.go_organic.com*.

*Goodwill
Close*

I hope to see you soon!

Sincerely,

Kathy George, Manager, Go Organic
kathygeorge@go_organic.com

*T*ools

Pay attention to how you load your sentences

Sentence loading is the key to a graceful sentence. But what is meant by "sentence loading"? If you're told to load the car, you'll probably put the heaviest items on bottom, the lighter ones on top, and arrange it all so that you can see clearly out all the windows. You don't put glassware on the bottom and hope it can support cartons of books!

Sentence loading is a little bit like that: You want to structure the sentence so it can hold all the information. You want to arrange the information logically. And you don't want the sentence to draw attention to the way it's written; you want the reader to just read, without getting hung up on awkward language or worse yet, pausing to wonder what the writer meant.

Learn to recognize a correctly loaded sentence

Consider this sentence: "Gourmet Lunchboxes are being discounted at 10% by Go Organic for all full-time employees of Vector, Inc." It seems a bit clunky, right? That's because none of the parts are in the right place. The passive verb tense ("are being discounted") throws the whole sentence out of whack.

Now look at this one: "I would like to extend to all the full-time employees of Vector, Inc. a 10% discount on Gourmet Lunchboxes." This sentence is better—there's a clear subject, an active verb, and the information is loaded in the complement at the end. But some of the bits in the complement aren't in the right order.

And finally: "I would like to extend a 10% discount on Gourmet Lunchboxes to all full-time Vector, Inc. employees." This sentence follows one of the normal loading patterns in English: I (subject) + would like to extend (active and polite verb tense) + a 10% discount on Gourmet Lunchboxes (direct object) + to all full-time Vector, Inc. employees (indirect object).

Shuffle the information around

First, locate the subject and pull it up front. Then put the verb next to it. Then build the complement out on the end. The direct object goes first (the bit that receives the action from the verb), followed by the indirect object (often preceded by a preposition).

Stay out of trouble by avoiding passive verb phrases

Active verbs, active readers! Passive verbs, bored readers. Passives are a big no-no in most writing contexts because they lead to heavy, sometimes convoluted, sentences.

How do you recognize a passive verb phrase? The usual tip-offs include: a noun at the beginning of the sentence that is receiving an action, rather than authoring an action; a to-be verb in the verb phrase; and a prepositional phrase at the end, usually prefaced by "by" or "in."

"The discount was offered by the manager" is passive; "The manager offered the discount" is active. "A salad is being featured in the Lunchbox" is passive; "The Lunchbox featured a salad" is active.

Of course, sometimes we do need to have a passive verb tense, but those occasions are rare. The professional rule-of-thumb is to change a passive into an active whenever you can.

Writing as sport

The first time you try to hold a new pose in your yoga class, you realize how difficult it is. The pose is still difficult the next few times, but each time you try it, you increase your ability to do it well in the future. The day finally comes when you can do it really well. Eventually, it's automatic.

The same holds true for writing. The learning curve can be steep for some at the beginning. But if you are determined to obtain a competitive edge, the initial effort will pay off. It gets easier. And then it's automatic.

Targeted Product Launch

Subject
Announcement

Product Need

Product Solution

Product
Application

Logistics

Goodwill
Close

Frank, Allen, Joanne,

As key members of Research and Development at Vector, Inc., you know just how prevalent electronic emissions are in the workplace. You also know electronic emissions are becoming an important public health issue. And you are probably aware of evidence that continued exposure to LANS reduces worker productivity.

Methods for monitoring electronic emissions (E-E) in the workplace are expensive and cumbersome. Many companies postpone purchasing an E-E monitoring system—even at the risk of employee health.

With the introduction of the Zyztem Electronic Emissions Reader—EER, for short—that situation is changing. The EER is portable, affordable and accurate. The size of a paperback book, the EER discretely sits on a desk, providing a continual read-out of emission levels. This information is stored in a memory stick with easy interface.

Because EER provides companies with the information they need to protect worker health, it helps maximize worker productivity. An accurate E-E monitoring system allows employers to pinpoint peak emissions in order to reroute services to less congested posts.

The EER specs are attached. For more information, please feel free to consult our Website at: *www.zyztem.com*.

Thank you for your time and attention.

Sincerely,

Robert Creel
EER Sales Manager
Zyztem International
robertcreel@zyztem.com

Tools

Flatter the readers in a "you" series

One of the easiest ways of getting the readers' attention is to pay tribute to their knowledge and authority. Come up with 2 to 4 sentences that feature "you," as in, "You know X. And you know Y. And you are probably aware of Z." A flattered reader is likely to be a receptive reader.

And because the "you" can't function without an implied "me," the "you" series humanizes the e-mail. It reinforces that a real person is writing the e-mail to real readers on the other end—or at least pretends to be.

Raise the reader's anxiety through presentation of worrisome facts

Sales professionals know that people are more apt to reach into their checkbooks to avoid pain than to procure pleasure. Tell the reader what the problem is that your product perfectly addresses. Keep your language direct and neutral, but not flat. Scientific objectivity is associated with a straightforward, precise tone. If you've chosen your facts carefully, they'll speak for themselves.

Announce that there's a solution for the problem

Once you've established that your readers are smart people who are aware of a pressing problem, deliver the solution that they want. Describe how your product works and what it will accomplish. Then tell them how to obtain additional information.

Netiquette

Of course it's a great idea to include a link to your company's Website in an e-mail. But be careful! You don't want the links to sprout up all over the place like weeds. Too many links give the reader too many choices. In many cases, it's better to send readers to the site and let them self-navigate. They may not look at every single thing you want them to look at, but they won't if you list each Webpage in your e-mail, either. If your site is well constructed, they'll find the information they need on their own.

In fact, some studies show that the more links you put in an e-mail, the less likely it is that the reader will click on them. It's better to go with one main link and keep your chances high.

Launch Announcement

Subject
Announcement

Product

Context

Follow-Up

Touch infinity.

Vector Dimensional Poetics System 5.9 is ready to download!

The flexibility you've come to expect from Vector Poetics, but with the brand-new 3rd-Millenium Enhancement.

Poetics 5.9:

- networks word, image, sound and layout applications
- provides instant, uncorrupted file exchange
- resolves format, platform and compatibility problems
- features voice recognition with global programming syntax
- offers virtual memory reload with real-time range and depth
- guarantees reduplicated script layering and replay
- fosters perceptive intuition, tightening feedback loops
- interfaces with PC, Mac, Pod, Blackberry, GPD and other equipment

With Poetics 5.9, your data is finally fluid—from your fingertips to the stars.

Check out *www.vector.com/poetics* or visit our nearest showroom.

$\mathcal{T}$ools

Drop the salutation and emphasize the lead in a launch announcement

The lead highlights the concept of the product in a catchy way. Make the lead titillating. You want to pique the reader's interest—not explain why the reader should be interested. You have to intrigue the reader first, then explain. Thus the lead "leads" the reader to the next sentence.

Always make a quick "why now" argument

Relevance is key in terms of catching—and holding—the reader's attention. Readers easily feel as if they've been left behind in the race to keep up with what's new. Product launches appeal to this anxiety: "What? You didn't know this product was on the market?"

Because "new" is often a synonym for "better," new items are more attractive, captivating, useful, and interesting than "old" items. The reader would have to prefer the newer product, right? Then tell the readers that the product is now available, just out on the market, just released, and so on. You'll play right into the consumer's need to keep up with the trends.

Link the new product to established products

A friend of a friend is more trustworthy than a stranger, right? The same thing holds true for products—the reader is apt to be interested in a new product that can rub elbows with established products. Situating the new product in the context of known product lines gives the reader an instant way of sizing-up quality and performance.

Favor verbs in a product description

Select the verbs in the product launch carefully. Use zesty, positive-spin verbs associated with the concept. Choose verbs that are part of the buzz— that amorphous, cultural climate in which has-beens and must-haves are decided. Or consider using verbs based on the readers' expectations regarding the product performance.

Frame the announcement with the product concept

Mentioning the same idea at the beginning and end of a text is called framing. The framing technique is popular because it: (1) reinforces the message and (2) makes the text seem solid and complete. Because the beginning and end mirror each other, they form a pair of sturdy bookends. By framing a product announcement with the concept, you maintain focus on product differentiation.

Marketing Query

Subject
Announcement

Announcement of Success

Future plan

Request for Referrals

Goodwill Close

Anne, Alice,

Can you please help us?

As you know, the Zyztem Electronic Emissions Reader (EER) has recently been chosen as "Innovative Product of the Year" by the Federation of Consumers for a Sustainable Environment.

This award brings enormous satisfaction to the EER team here at Zyztem and heralds a new push for expansion in the field of IT consumer protection. We plan on doubling production of the EER in the first quarter of 2008, when we will also launch a new line of EERs for home use.

Because you are satisfied customers of the EER product, we would like to know if you could suggest e-colleagues who might benefit from our services? Referrals from the chief purchasing agents at Vector, Inc. will help us reach individuals and companies who need our products and services.

Please know that we value your comments and suggestions.

Sincerely,

Robert Creel
EER Sales Manager
Zyztem International
robertcreel@zyztem.com

Tools

Use questions to arouse the reader's interest

A question is a quick, reliable way to get the reader's attention. Why? Because a lifetime of language experience has taught the reader that a question has an answer. As the question echoes in the reader's mind, it arouses curiosity. With an almost Pavlovian response, the reader must read on to find the reply. Instinct, anticipation, and suspense all come into play—provided the question is interesting.

Use rhetorical questions to emphasize the writer's authority

If an e-mail begins with the question, "What were the real reasons behind the plummeting stock market in 2007?" the reader might have a tentative answer or none at all. He or she will have to read on to find a satisfactory response, even if that response is open-ended. Questions that readers can't adequately answer by themselves put the writer's knowledge and authority in the limelight.

Use literal questions to emphasize the reader's authority

When the writer asks the reader a question that only the reader has the answer to, the writer pays tribute to the reader's decision-making power. For example, "Will you help us?" can't be answered by the writer—only the reader can reply. Depending on the specificity of the question, the readers can be flattered, worried, alerted, or even feel superior with the power assigned to them. The trick is for the writer to channel that energy into a desired outcome.

Use questions to emphasize the you/me relationship between reader and writer

Questions emphasize the productive bond between the writer and reader. When someone asks a question, usually someone answers it. Writers can emphasize the you-and-me aspect of questions by literally putting the pronouns into play. In the question "Have you heard about the recent nanotech innovation?" the writer seems to directly address the reader. Here, as elsewhere, the you-and-me feature humanizes the e-mail. It's not just words projected impersonally on a screen. It's the writer and reader, participating in a communication exchange, each complementing the other.

Trying putting questions in different places in a text

Questions can occur in the subject line. Or you could put one at the start of the opening paragraph. As headers, questions allow you to organize a text at the same time that you prime the reader's interest. A question at the conclusion of text has dramatic power, doesn't it?

Options

Please know that we value your comments and suggestions...

Please know that your feedback means a lot to us...

Meeting your business needs is our priority...

Thank you for your continued support...

We are grateful for your loyalty...

We appreciate your interest and support...

We are pleased to number you among our valued clients...

Your business is very important us, both now and in the future...

Readers like to be welcomed

When you visit someone's home, you like to be greeted at the door, ushered inside, and given refreshments. You like to have a nice place to sit, and close friends with whom to talk.

You don't feel as welcome if you have to open the door yourself, find your own way to the living room, and move the laundry off the couch to sit down. You don't feel welcomed if you find out that there's nothing to drink or eat, and if your host takes phone calls throughout the visit.

Think of the reader as your guest. If the e-mail is structured to encourage reading facility, if it's cleaned up to avoid confusion, and if the main points are clear, the reader will feel that he or she has been taken care of. If the e-mail is substandard, the reader will feel neglected...or even angry.

$\mathcal{E}$dit

Before: status of marketing research

Hey Girls,

The E-Hotels marketing survey, recently completed, is in the process of being analyzed by the team here at Vector, Inc.
as you'll see in the results in the executive summary and full report, which are going to be sent to you soon.

In conclusion, the E-Hotels Survey is below our expectation, as we will be discussing at Heathrow. Of course the data are being gone through to get at whatever is of use.

The vendor Real People was not apparently being supervised as well as we had hoped by our in-house delegate so that the questions are not ideal. We got a lot of data but not the exact information that we were looking for though some of it is useful.

The coming days I'll be setting up a conference call so we can discuss.

Regards,

T. S. Loringhoven
General Marketing Operations Associate
Vector, Inc.
tsloringhoven@vector.com

The problems

Layout! The atypical indentations stymie the reader from the get-go. Indented information is supposed to be *intentional*, not haphazard. Indents map the document for the reader, so that the more specific the information is, the more indented it is. Can you figure out the hierarchy of information from the layout? Nope.

Sentence Order! The order of the sentences in a document and in a paragraph is supposed to reinforce the hierarchy of information, not confuse it even more. In this e-mail, sentence order isn't doing its job. You can read the e-mail through without even being sure what the main points are. That's an ineffective e-mail, indeed.

Passive verb tenses! Look at all the "being" and "by" words. When used together, "being" and "by" set up a passive verb construction, which usually means that the sentence is heavy, long, and unclear. Instead of the subject acting on the verb, the subject, is well, being acted upon—the difference between "I kissed my lover" and "I was kissed by my lover," to put it bluntly. The passive tense is the quickest way to turn an efficient and active e-mail into a dull and slow one.

The solution

Lose the indentations—they belong to the old hardcopy days and, with the exception of an elegant list or two, render scant service to the business e-mail. In some e-mail programs, indentations take on a life of their own, moving around the page and/or transforming themselves into gobbledygook. Put your indentations in your attachments if need be, but make certain they reinforce the hierarchy of idea, not lobby against it.

Lead with the most important information. You want your main points to shine at the start of the e-mail and at the start of each paragraph. Pulling your main point up to the top furthers clarity and saves time. It helps writers stay on track and helps readers skim for information that they want. That way, the reader won't get frustrated reading and rereading— and you won't have to write a second e-mail explaining what you should have written clearly the first time around.

Get rid of the "being" and "by" combination. Just by removing the word "being," you're forced to transform a passive-verb sentence and make it active. And an active sentence is more pleasurable to read, more memorable, and more likely to be clear. As we say in the trade: active verb, active sentence; active sentence, active reader.

You're more visible in e-mail than in person
The higher-ups remember who takes the time to write a clear and effective e-mail.

And they remember who doesn't.

After: status of marketing research

Marianne, Laura, Norine, Mina,

As you know, the Vector, Inc. Marketing Research Team, headed by Tristan Betton, is analyzing the recently completed E-Hotels Marketing Survey. Unfortunately, our primary market research questions resulted in significant qualitative flaws.

Tristan, our in-house delegate, under-supervised the vendor Real People. Consequently, the probing psychographics focused on follow-ups at the expense of closed-ends. Length and sequencing were against us—we covered a lot of terrain but without much depth.

Overall, the E-Hotels Survey is disappointing, as we will discuss at our monthly meeting at Heathrow on August 12. I wanted to give you the heads-up before the executive summary and full report reach your offices by the end of next week. Please know that I am working to salvage whatever information data we can.

I'll set up a conference call in the coming days so we can come up with a game plan.

Regards,

T. S. Loringhoven
General Marketing Operations Associate
Vector, Inc.
tsloringhoven@vector.com

Tools

Always say clearly *why* you're writing—right away

It's the simplest thing to do, and the one most likely to be omitted. Remember: Your reader wants to know clearly why you're writing in the first couple of lines. Everything else in the e-mail is just supporting information.

Use a direct, authoritative tone

Business e-mails aren't about making friends, showing how cool you are, or parading the fancy vocabulary you know. Business e-mails are about business. Toward that end, state your business clearly and directly. An authoritative tone and style come across, even when readers don't understand insider jargon. And when you have bad news, you want to take even more time to write it well.

When the news is bad, include a plan

In business, quitters and complainers are docked, fighters and warriors rewarded. Business is, after all, about action—and action is the best remedy for disappointing news. When you're the one who has to break the bad news, do it quickly, without hedging, and immediately follow-up with suggestions to correct or compensate for the untoward situation. The disappointing side to your message will be bolstered by your ready resolve.

When going through your inbox, look at your email to see:

—Which e-mail has more authority?

—Which e-mail suggests the situation is under control?

—Which one looks sloppy?

—Which e-mail lends itself to rapid comprehension?

—Which one seems unsure and uncertain?

—Which e-mail seems centered on the reader?

CHAPTER SIX

Working as a Team

INCLUDING

Congratulations

Change in Policy

Explaining a Procedure

Encouraging Teamwork

Employee Training

Company Reception

Congratulations

Subject
Announcement

Situation

Triumph

Reason

Personal
Appreciation

Lyn, Carla, Barry, Bob, Ron,

I want to say that it was great working with you and your teams on the Lumina Corp. closing.

As we know, this was one of the most difficult closings in Vector history. It wasn't just the deal on the table, but the direction—and even the future—of our firm in the next 10 years. We weren't negotiating for value and profits—we were negotiating for every employee and for every investor, from the loading dock to the boardroom.

And we succeeded! When we were at the table in Boston with experts in French and German law, we never missed a beat and achieved our goals without significant compromise. We more than matched the hordes of experts directed at us by Lumina, even when the employee compensation issues hit us broadside.

Throughout this difficult time, you delivered selfless, unhesitating support. You were available at all hours, even well after midnight on the Memorial Day weekend; you responded quickly to every deadline, including the last-minute TAP; and you proved that your knowledge and understanding of the issues, from R&D through MIS, are outstanding.

I couldn't be more proud of the Vector negotiations team.

Regards,

Dave Bromige
Chief Information Officer
Vector, Inc.
davebromige@vector.com

Tools

Personalize to really show the team your appreciation

Personalization begins with a liberal use of the first and second person pronouns—I, we, and you. If there's an "I" and "you," there's also a "we"—people sending and receiving e-mail on their computers, people who work together. Even if you're thanking the team on behalf of the firm, personalize the message by humanizing the language.

Although pronouns allow you to emphasize human bonds between team members, that doesn't mean you're all on the same level. You can keep your "I" in a position of authority while praising the "you." The trick is endowing the "I" with observations that only someone in authority can make.

Include a specific example of an accomplishment

An e-mail of congratulations, commendation, and thanks requires specific examples—otherwise, it's just the same old stuff. Specificity is what makes one laudatory e-mail different from another.

By taking the time to point out an example of what the team did, you show them that their contribution was noted, both at the time and later in writing. Specific examples allow you to draw attention to qualities and actions that separate your readers from the pack.

Use parallel structure to pack information into a sentence

Parallel structure is a nifty way of stuffing info into an e-mail. In writing, "parallel" means something similar to "consistency"—words, phrases, clauses, or parts of the sentence that are structured the same way.

Here are some examples of parallel structures you can use:

You were X, Y, and Z.

You were W. You were X. You were Y. And you were Z.

You were X, you were Y, and you were Z.

A successful parallel sentence has consistent structure. The base "You did" doesn't vary, while the W, X, Y, Z keep the same grammar, but the content differs. For example, the W, X, Y, and Z could all be nouns, noun phrases, or verb phrases.

You were dedicated, determined, and knowledgeable.

You were dedicated to the team's objectives. You were determined to meet every deadline. You were knowledgeable about the fine point of business. And you were prepared to meet every objection.

You were dedicated to the team's objectives, you were determined to meet every deadline, and you were prepared to meet every objection.

The more you master parallel structure, the more zing and flair your e-mails will have.

*I*nbox

If you've done a good job, more than anything else, you want to be recognized! One of the key factors in job satisfaction is recognition—the boss noticed I worked overtime, the boss noticed I got the account back, the boss noticed how much my presentations have improved, and so on. That's why in a "Congratulations" e-mail, specificity is so important.

Change in Policy

Chris, Louis, Jenny, Wallace, and Rolph,

Subject
Announcement

As members of the cross-functional Oversight Task Force, you are responsible for implementing the Strategy for Improved Phone Security (SIPS) in your assignments. You should familiarize yourselves with the full extent of the policy posted on the intranet: *www.vector.com/dimensional/voicephone*.

Obligation

Before June 11:

Former Policy

Company cell phones are used strictly for company business. During breaks and lunch hour, there is no restriction on the usage of personal cell phones.

After June 11:

Current Policy

Employees will open and close thier business phone lines at the beginning and end of the workday using voice-activated security codes. Caps on personal use are unchanged.

Required Step

To file a voice-activated code, employees must follow the log-in instructions posted on the intranet. The Help Desk at Vector will be able to assist employees with the procedure.

Phone Number Recognition Data will automatically keep track of personal call volume. We will also have precise records of the number of calls and their business destinations.

Please emphasize to your reports that SIPS is designed to protect them from fraudulent use of their lines. Once we have an accurate database of phone records, we'll be able to reduce abuse of the company phones.

Goodwill Close

Feel free to contact me with your concerns.

Regards,

Stanley Lake
Information Security Director
Vector, Inc.
stanlake@vector.com

$\mathcal{T}$ools

Take a moment to consider the modals

Modals are a special group of old verbs—"old" in the sense that they recall a distant moment in the evolution of the English language. If you've had a chance to look at them closely, you'll know they're weird. For example, "will" is a present-tense modal; "would" is past tense. But it doesn't seem as clear-cut as saying that "walks" is present tense and "walked" is past tense, does it?

Despite their odd morphology, modal verbs are frequently used in English. Even nonnative speakers quickly get the hang of them because we use them so often. For the record, official modal verbs include: can/could, may/might, will/would, shall/should, and must. "Have," "ought," and a few other stragglers are sometimes included in the list as "semi-modals."

Don't overuse the modals

Just because we use them frequently, doesn't mean we have to use them all the time. If you don't have a clear reason for using a modal, opt for a simple verb. Instead of, "I would phone frequently," try "I phoned frequently." Nonnative speakers of English are especially tempted to use a modal when a simple verb will do. So are writers who are not confident in their writing skills.

Select the right modal for the occasion

Most of us choose our modal verbs by instinct alone. No wonder! Not even top grammarians agree on the "meaning" of the modals. Generally speaking, modals have to do with the likelihood of an action being accomplished. Modals provide a predictive scale of accomplishment, from highly unlikely to reasonably certain.

Possible: You might log-on (it's really up to you if you want to or not).

Possible: You could log-on (it depends on whether you have the desire and the ability).

Probable: You may log-on (it's your decision; nothing will stop you).

Obligation: You should log-on (you are obliged to, whether you want to or not).

Strong Obligation: You have to log-on (you don't have much choice).

Necessity: You must log-on (you don't have any choice about it at all).

Certainty: You will log-on (it's a done deal).

Use modal verbs when you want to be polite

The evolution of the English language has endowed past-tense modals (could, might, would, should) with social graces. The past tense modal is more polite than the present tense. And "would" when used in a question is the politest of all.

Consider the following. "Explain it to me," gives an order. "Will you explain it to me?" ostensibly gives the reader a chance to refuse, but still keeps the writer in the driver's seat. But in "Would you explain it to me?" the writer is humbled, or making a polite request up the chain of command.

Avoid using "ought" and "shall"

These two words are used more frequently in British English than in American English, but even in the UK, their usage is arguably in decline. They sound nostalgic and quaint. You want to sound sharp and up-to-date.

Netiquette

E-mail favors starting sentences with "And," "But," or "Or." If you were taught that this is a no-no, it's time to move on. The English language evolves rapidly, and you have to move with it, or you risk looking old-fashioned when you want to be forward thinking.

Because e-mail is one of the most rapidly evolving arenas for language use, we'd expect to find evidence of innovation. It's no surprise then to observe the proliferation of sentences starting with conjunctions in e-mail documents. And we can probably expect this pattern to impact initial conjunctions in hardcopy, too. They're on the rise in print media, and even in rulings by Supreme Court Justices.

Conjunctions are handy ways of starting sentences because they emphasize links. In other words, "And" is used to announce additional information. "But" is used to cue the reader into an objection, while "or" suggests an alternative. These words, however, don't always have to start a sentence. They can also be used inside a sentence. Making the decision as to whether or not you want to start a sentence with the conjunction or subsume it in a larger unit depends on whether the conjunction is worthy of emphasis.

In the sentence, "I think so, but I'm not sure," the objection is less emphatic than "I think so. But I'm not sure."

Explaining a Procedure

Subject Announcement

Dear Chem-Lab Team,

As we discussed in the weekly R&D meeting, visitors to the labs must adhere to new procedures. Effective immediately:

First Step

1) The visitor's name and ID information must be filed on the Vector Security Clearance Site (VSCS).

Second Step

2) The "Visitor Clearance Request Form" (VSCS-348X) must be completed at least two working days prior to the visit.

Third Step

3) The form must briefly describe the reason for the visit (required clearances will be pulled up automatically).

Fourth Step

4) A copy of the Visitor Clearance Request Form will be sent to your supervisor for approval, and you will be notified of the result.

Fifth Step

5) If your supervisor approves the visit and security clearances are met, you will be asked to fill out an "On-Site Visitor Form" (349X) also available on VSCS.

Sixth Step

6) Upon arrival at Vector Labs, the visitor will be required to present identification. He or she will also be required to submit to a mandatory search, including pat-down.

Seventh Step

7) A security escort will be assigned to the visitor for the duration of the visit.

Goodwill Close

If you have any questions about the new procedure, please contact me or visit VSCS for more information.

Regards,

Duncan McGiver
Director, Vector Chemical Laboratories
Vector Dimensional
duncanmcgiver@vector.com

Tools

Maintain an authoritative tone in notices

When you make a request, you try to be polite because it's at the reader's discretion to decide when and how to respond. Not so with a company's policies and procedures. A "policy" refers to a change in strategy. A "procedure" refers to specific guidelines. Although sometimes they're used interchangeably, there's nothing optional about either of them. All the more reason to opt for a firm, direct tone when introducing them to your reports.

List the sequential steps in the procedure

Because notification of procedures has required outcomes, you want to communicate the steps as clearly and precisely as you possibly can. One way of maintaining clarity is by articulating a strict, sequential order...which is often easier to say than to do!

To avoid confusion and keep the order clear, the best technique is to break down sequential steps of a procedure into small increments. That way you'll write more clearly, and the reader will have a better chance of instantly comprehending the company's expectations.

Try not to clutter your procedural memo

While it's tempting to write in a kind of acronymic shorthand, avoid it in a procedural memo. You're trying to get the employees to behave a certain way to avoid having to correct them in the future. The odds of success increase if you formalize the language a little more than you normally would—formality is another means of expressing gravity. Spell out the acronym at first mention, even for the old-timers, and follow it by the abbreviation. High formality in style correlates with legality in content. Therefore, just by adopting a more formal, serious tone than you do in other e-mail correspondence, you subtly emphasize that this procedure is official—and to be followed. It's company law, so to speak. No exceptions.

Writing a bicycle

Writing effectively is a skill that can be taught. Top e-mail skill doesn't require innate talent or a lengthy apprenticeship. Once you learn, you always know how to do it.

*N*etiquette

Business e-mail is suited to parenthesis. Along with the increase in sentence fragments and sentences starting with conjunctions, parentheses are arguably getting more play in e-mail than they are in hardcopy. Often overlooked as marks of punctuation, parentheses provide a handy, concise way of expanding, explaining, or commenting on a point you've already made.

In "Vector Security Clearance Site (VSCS)," the parenthetical acronym tells the reader that the abbreviation will be used in the rest of the document. Rather than saying, "I'm going to use this acronym from now on," the writer just puts the abbreviation in parenthesis.

Similarly, in "On-Site Visitor Form (349X)," the parentheses succinctly explain that the form has a number and that the number is 349X. And in "The form must briefly, but clearly, describe the reason for the visit (required clearances will be pulled up automatically)," the parentheses supply supplementary information without obliging the writer to take the time to structure a new sentence with an explicit link.

Parentheses imply connections that don't have to be stated outright. Consequently, they're a natural in a communication medium that is constantly looking to cut corners without sacrificing clarity.

The style sheet

Some companies have specific writing guidelines for their employees to use. A list of writing *do's* and *don'ts* is called a *style sheet*. Not so long ago, many companies had a style sheet for secretaries to follow. Once personal secretaries were phased out and executives were largely responsible for their own correspondence, style sheets fell into disuse. Now they are making a comeback.

If your company does not have a style sheet, keep examples of different kinds of correspondence in your *style file* for future reference. These examples can be used as models when you have to write your own letters.

Encouraging Teamwork

Jack, Lew,

Subject Announcement

I am writing to tell you that I need your support on the Lumina Allied team now more than ever.

Problem

As you know, the IPO market has been hard hit in recent weeks, exactly when we're preparing to go public. I am concerned that our can-do attitude is being replaced by a couldn't-do—right at the time we need to carry the ball over the line and score!

Solution

Market trends are just that—market trends. They come, they go. We need to keep in mind that we're not just selling a product—we're selling to someone. That is the message I want you to pass to your teams: Who we're selling to counts just as much as what we're selling.

Outcome

And that's exactly why we're going to win. Our investors believe in our product, but they also believe they're backing the best team. In fact, they believe in us so much that the subscriptions are being snapped up. We have to try as hard as we can in this final hour to get to the finish line and win.

Goodwill Close

I'll see you at the 2:30 meeting later today.

Regards,

Robin Brune
Chief Information Officer
Lumina Allied
robinbrune@lumina.com

$\mathcal{T}$ools

Add verve to business e-mail with metaphors

Business e-mail, as with other writing forms, is obliged to emphasize the rational over the affective, the logical over the emotional, the impassive over the expressive. But in some cases, we need a little punch—we need to touch the readers' feelings as much as their thoughts—particularly when we need to motivate or persuade them to do something.

Enter the metaphor, with its compact emotional appeal. Metaphors function as a kind of compressed shorthand for a complex of ideas. If you say, "the sales reps huddled before the presentation," instead of "the sales reps spoke together before the presentation" you send two very different signals. One is bursting with positive messages; the other is much more restrained and bland.

Because teams "huddle," the verb suggests that they're working together, and because a huddle has to do with strategy, it suggests that the reps are working on a successful approach to a problem. A huddle connotes secrecy; we assume that the reps have some sort of special knowledge. And because a huddle occurs before play begins, we know the reps are preparing for action. A huddle usually excludes those not in the game, so we know that the reps are among the chosen. And a huddle requires agreement, which tells us that the reps will put loyalty to the company before their differences among one another.

That's a lot of information supplied by one word!

Choose your metaphors carefully

Business e-mail favors sports and war metaphors. It routinely excludes metaphors based on gardens, on marine life, and/or on celestial bodies. Nature metaphors belong to the *boudoir*, not to the boardroom.

Consider, for example, how often you see the following words or phrases in business English: teamwork, team player, score, pass the ball, step up to the plate, play hardball, play fair, tackle a problem, give a play-by-play, ante-up, put your cards on the table, hit the basket, take the ball and run with it, steal the ball, strike out, commit a foul, get called out, rack up points, play the field, hit a home run, par for the course, tee up, and so on.

Or think of these: on the offense, on the defense, close ranks, call in the back-up, do double-duty, move to the front lines, or speak to the commander. Or even drop the bomb, get the ammo out, take down the leader, explode the ranks, stab him in the back, get a shot, shoot to kill, bleed an account, take territory, take 'em down, kill 'em, throttle them, straggle them, explode them out of the water, sink the ship, go for the throat, show no mercy, nail 'em, nuke 'em, and so on.

Sports and war metaphors are based on opposition. There's a "we" on one side, and a "them" on the other. The relationship between the two is adversarial—somebody has to win, somebody has to lose (or live or die). In business, it usually isn't points or casualties or even territory that's really at stake. The fight is for money. Or power. Or both.

Use business metaphors to express feelings that can't be expressed any other way

It would be difficult, if not impossible, for most managers to tell their reports, "I really feel good working with you." But it's easy to say, "Good news! You're defending the front lines, Paul." To some degree, sports and war metaphors allow writers to voice their joy, sorrow, affection, and anger without being singled out for unconventional behavior. In a context where conformity receives the highest value, you don't want to stand out for violating a communication code that places a heavy premium on masking feelings rather than showing them.

Use business metaphors to emphasize the collective enterprise

With their built-in emphasis on teamwork, sports and war metaphors remind us that business is always a group effort in which winning, even survival itself, depends on working well together.

Structure as a shortcut

Most writers lose time trying to figure out where to put information in an e-mail. Because they don't know where a particular point goes, they tend to repeat it, hoping that it will land in the right place. Worse yet, they might omit crucial information because poor document organization led them astray. The figure-it-out-as-you-go strategy to organization is ineffective and counterproductive. It's better to take 5 extra minutes to identify the main points than to casually hunt for them.

Employee Training

Subject
Announcement

Problem

Next Steps

Solution

Goodwill
Close

All,

As part of its commitment to lifelong learning, Vector, Inc., is holding a writing training session on November 6–9, 2007 at the Renaissance Ramada (*www.vector.com/training/e-mail*).

For sometime, upper management has been discussing our firm's need for clear and efficient e-mail communication. Spot-checks of e-mail messages frankly reveal an appalling state of affairs. Just because an employee is literate, doesn't mean he or she writes well. Many of you have been told that your promotions are partially contingent on improvement in written communication skills.

The writing seminar will address the e-mail forms and issues specific to our company. Managers have been asked to collect sample e-mail from their reports. These e-mails will be filtered for confidentiality and used as the basis of discussion during the seminar. If you have particular pieces of writing on file that you'd like to have considered for discussion, please forward them to me.

At the seminar you'll be trained to spot your own writing weakness and learn to correct them. You will be provided with tools for assessment and evaluation. You will improve your writing, no matter what level of skill you possess. Together we'll learn to streamline our written communications—reducing both inbox volume and miscommunications. And free-up more of our time for making our business grow!

I look forward to seeing you there.

Regards,

T. Raymond Hobson
Executive Manager, Business Unit
Vector, Inc.
traymondhobson@vector.com

 ## Tools

Use criticism as a tool of motivation, but do so carefully

Meek, hesitant criticism is usually not taken seriously—it's apt to be dismissed as misguided. Strong, perhaps vicious, criticism also isn't effective. It will probably be rejected as too extreme. Your best bet is to strike a middle ground, explaining what the problem is in direct, matter-of-fact, statements. Then it's likely that your criticism will at least be heard, if not acted on.

Use other "authorities" to boost your case

If you are supported not just by one manager, but the united front of upper management, your case has more weight. Because then, if readers disagree with you, they'll have to disagree with everyone else, too. Faced with overwhelming resistance, the opposition usually backs down.

Although referring to the higher peaks of the orgizational chart usually works, you can also call upon one key person in the news or in history, provided he or she is held in respect or awe by your readers, for example, "if it was good enough for Henry Ford, it's good enough for me." But remember, historical figures are generally less persuasive than a well-known person currently in the limelight. And the firm's own decision makers are often best of all.

> ### Forget your past writing instruction
>
> Some writing teachers have a gift that allows them to tailor their ideas exactly to the student's needs; others seem to have a knack for saying the wrong thing, and then wonder why the student doesn't make progress.
>
> Many business professionals carry around writing criticism they received in their youth like some sort of dirty secret. They harbor negative criticism for decades and allow it to sabotage them in the present. Remember that the writing criticism you've received in the past emerged from a specific context that is no longer relevant to the business professional you've become.

Make sure the benefits are clear

If you want employees to do something without anger or resentment, take time to appeal to their self-interest. Ensure compliance and goodwill by explaining how a particular course of action will result in personal gain.

Use mild threats to cinch your case

Do-it-or-else has worked from time immemorial and still works today, provided that the team has a clear idea of what the consequences are. These consequences should be real and quantifiable; empty, unclear threats are useless and provide evidence of inconsistency and indecisiveness. For example, "Many of you have been told that your promotions are partially contingent on improvement in written communication skills" gets the job done, while "we all need to improve our writing, or else!" doesn't.

Ensure the readers that you're following your own advice

A general who fights side-by-side with his or her soldiers earns respect. For example, it's difficult to persuade employees of the benefits of a particular course of action if you wouldn't follow it yourself.

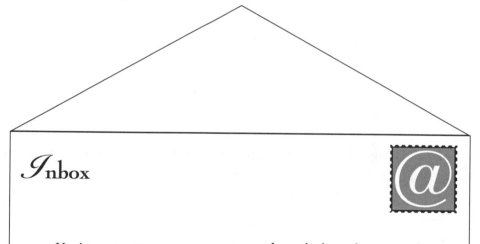

*I*nbox

You've just gotten an announcement from the boss about attending a seminar that you don't want to go to. You want to be persuaded, even convinced, about the payback. Persuasion appeals more to the reader's emotions, while conviction appeals more to logic. Ideally, you want to have both persuasion and conviction working together to achieve your objective. "You are capable of doing much better work" encourages you to take pride in your work, while "attending this seminar will help you get promoted" appeals to the rational logic of getting ahead.

Company Reception

Subject *Announcement*	Colleagues, Please join me in welcoming our new Human Resources Manager, Laura Morrison, on Friday, June 16, 5:00–7:00 pm, in Duncan Hall.
Background	Laura comes to Vector, Inc. from Rex Co., where she held the post of Chief Compensation Analyst. She brings to Vector a thorough understanding of our most vital asset: You. As Human Resources Manager, Laura will field your questions and concerns during this uncertain time of restructuring.
Goodwill *Close*	I look forward seeing you there. Sincerely, Alex Barron General Manager Vector, Inc. *alexbarron@vector.com*

𝒯ools

Avoid impersonal salutations

When you don't know the names of every reader, use the group name, such as "Team Members" and "Associates." Another option is to use "All." Avoid old-fashioned salutations, including "Gentlemen" and "Sir or Madame." Use "To Whom It May Concern" only when there's no other option.

Keep it short

E-mail encourages brevity—especially in employee-wide memos. Longer documents end up as attachments and/or posted on the intranet. For invitations or announcements, stick to the basics: who, what, when, where, and why.

Use "Sincerely" as a close instead of "Regards" to signal a social function

"Regards" is the all-purpose business e-mail close, but when the occasion lends itself to discussing the latest movies as much as the latest spread sheet, use "sincerely" instead.

𝒩etiquette

The sequence of information is more important in e-mail than it is in hardcopy. Hardcopy had the luxury of building suspense before it announced its main point. Not so in e-mail. Screen-based media by nature emphasizes the opening of the announcement, not its middle or its end. The opening is visible on screen when we open the document; the rest of the e-mail often isn't. The reader's behavior is usually determined by the impact of the first few lines.

Sequential emphasis on first things also applies to the syntax (word order) of the sentence. Consider how the following sentence is divvied up into incremental units in a descending order of importance: "Please join me in welcoming our new Human Resources Manager, Laura Morrison, on June 16, 5:00–7:00 pm, in Duncan Hall."

Please join me = the boss is making a request

in welcoming = the purpose of the event

our new Human Resources Manager, Laura Morrison = the person being honored

on Friday, June 16 = the day and date

5:00–7:00 pm = the time

in Duncan Hall = the place

This sentence is constructed so that the most important information comes first—a request from the boss—and ends in the room where the event is being held. In adhering to the pattern of descending order of importance, the sentence takes advantage of sequential emphasis. Most of the time, first things get more attention than last things.

Compare that example to the following: "In Duncan Hall, from 5:00 – 7:00 pm on Friday, June 16, our new Human Resources Manager, Laura Morrison will be welcomed by all of us."

In this example, Duncan Hall takes on the most importance—otherwise, why does it head the sentence? And the time must be more important than the date—otherwise, why would it precede? Finally we find out who the event is for, and lastly, that we're expected to be there. This sentence literally goes against the flow of English—and it shows.

Although occasionally professional writers deliberately violate sequential emphasis to achieve a specific stylistic effect, in a lot of business e-mail, a descending order of importance is the most efficient, and most effective, way of communicating.

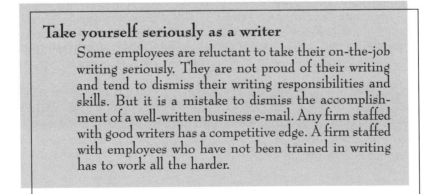

Take yourself seriously as a writer

Some employees are reluctant to take their on-the-job writing seriously. They are not proud of their writing and tend to dismiss their writing responsibilities and skills. But it is a mistake to dismiss the accomplishment of a well-written business e-mail. Any firm staffed with good writers has a competitive edge. A firm staffed with employees who have not been trained in writing has to work all the harder.

*A*dvice

Inclusive language

It's the final quarter of the last century—and business writing undergoes a revolutionary change. *Inclusive* language replaces exclusive language. Sexist words—and the gendered phraseology that goes along with them—flee from correspondence. American Business English becomes adamantly gender-neutral, and nonbiased.

For example, no one uses "Sirs" in a salutation anymore, unless the writer wants to send the message that he or she is from the old country. (And therefore, probably not the right person to do business with!) Similarly, no one wants to use "Oriental" for a man of Japanese origin. "Asian" is preferred, just as "disabled" is preferred over "handicapped." While at first glance some of these changes might appear as cosmetic, or even just fussy, they're not. If you want to change how people think, you have to change the language they use.

When writers who are accustomed to placing "Sir" at the top of a letter learn to replace it by "Dear Shipping Agent," they are doing more than sending a signal that they're up-to-date on inclusion trends. They're also acknowledging that a woman in authority might be reading the letter.

Inclusion, as with e-mail itself, has large numbers in mind. With the push of a button, an e-mail can hurtle through cyberspace into inboxes all over the globe; and the recipient can be female or male, adolescent or octogenarian, Korean or Kuwaiti, Canadian or Argentinean. Potential readers must *always* be kept in mind. Or to put it another way: Potential readers should always be *included*.

Anything that singles out a group or groups is a no-no. For this reason, jokes have no place in business e-mail. Dumb Blond jokes, for example, may seem harmless—unless you're blond and have spent a portion of your life fighting the stereotype. Just like midget jokes and stuttering jokes—humor at the expense of someone's physical identity is inappropriate, if not rude.

Similarly, what folks do when they're off work doesn't fully come into discussion at work. Sports, restaurants, shopping—these are safe coffee-machine fare. Who is sitting across from you at the breakfast table is not, neither is what you were doing in the wee hours the night before.

Although some corporate cultures try to exert influence even on their employees' time off, this is usually perceived as invasive in the Anglophone business world. As long as the employees are 100 percent at work, what they do when they're not in their cubicles is their own affair.

Do...

Use "he or she" or "him or her" when you *must* use a pronoun (if you can't use "they" or "them").

Opt for a group tag, such as "Purchasing Agents," when the recipients are unknown or too numerous to name. Or substitute a title, "Dear Customer Service Representative." If you know the name but not the gender, use "Dear R. Smith." If you're not sure what the person's professional identity is, then use "To Whom It May Concern" as a last resort.

Pick neutral replacements for gendered nouns whenever possible. For example, instead of "postman" use "postal worker." Instead of "stewardess," use "flight attendant."

Don't...

Ever assume that a male pronoun refers to both males and females in English, as it does in other languages.

Ever use the salutation, "Gentlemen," unless you want to insist on being from the old country.

Ever assume that gender issues are not serious enough to warrant careful attention.

Ever use "Miss"; it's considered demeaning. And don't use "Mrs." indiscriminately, unless you want to send the message that you're out-of-synch with the times.

CHAPTER SEVEN

Employee Issues

INCLUDING

Time for Promotion

Away From My Desk

Employee Transfer Request

Resignation

Problem in the Office

Thank You for the Bonus

Time for Promotion

Subject
Announcement

Yasmin,

As you know, Bob Halling plans to step down at Assistant Director of Management Information Systems in the coming month. After giving the matter careful thought, I would like to be considered for the position. Here are my reasons:

RESULTS

Results

In the 2 years that I've been at my post as Associate Manager of Strategic Marketing Communications, I pioneered the Vector, Inc. e-ads that resulted in <u>an unprecedented 12 percent upswing</u> in early adopters of Poetics 5.9.

MANAGEMENT

Management

I have a total of <u>16 reports</u>, including 2 direct team managers, 1 direct cross-functional manager, and 3 indirect team managers. I have also tightened the relationship with the Tactical Sales Department, initiating the <u>weekly cross-functional Web chat</u>.

VISION

Vision

I believe that Vector is posed to capture an additional 10 percent of the market share in Q2 and Q3. MIS is the kingpin of this expansion, provided that decentralization is accompanied by: (1) a strict unification of the Vector platform among departments, functions, and employees; (2) an understanding that documentation equates action; and (3) speed and flexibility of resources adapt to market trends.

Goodwill
Close

I welcome the opportunity to discuss my vision with you in more detail. I thank you for your attention.

Regards,

Levi Danes
Associate Manager of Strategic Marketing
Vector, Inc.
levidanes@vector.com

Tools

Add numbers to add creditability

For better or worse, readers have the impression that numbers can be trusted and words can't. Numbers are somehow thought to be more factual, more reliable. The number 10 is always the number 10, and 1.5 billion is always 1.5 billion. But what is meant by "competent"? Or "successful"? Or even a more banal term, such as "punctual"?

Words are context-sensitive—their meaning is dependent on the context in which they're found. The sentence, the paragraph, the text, and the sequence in which a document is read all influence a word's meaning. Its connotations are also dependent on the writer and reader, what their likes and dislikes are, expectations, knowledge, disposition, and so on.

Use numbers to persuade

A reader who skims a text and sees a lot of numbers receives the message that the text is objective and factual. As he or she reads more slowly, the numbers literally accumulate as the text insists that it can be relied on and trusted.

Try using Arabic numbers instead of number words whenever you can. Instead of "four years at my post" make it "4 years at my post." Instead of "moved from the fifth rank to the fourth," try "moved from number 5 to number 4."

Also, don't forget to structure your sentences, when appropriate, with sequential points, such as (1), (2), and (3). You'll not only speed up the reader's comprehension, you'll also be sending the message that what you're saying is logical, reliable, and true.

Use Arabic numbers to save time

"Three-hundred and thirty-three thousand seven-hundred and forty-eight" may be necessary for contracts, but in other contexts, it's a waste of time—and a bit weird. "333,748" will do. Similarly, "The meeting is at four o'clock" is more efficiently written as, "The meeting is at 4 PM." And even "I phoned five times" is often better in e-mail as "I phoned 5 times."

As e-mail evolves into a medium of even greater rapidity and concision, even that major no-no of English grammar—"never start a sentence with Arabic numbers; always use number words"—may yield. We may be starting sentences with "10 new outlets have opened" with no risk whatsoever of being called down for an unprofessional presentation in prose.

Away From My Desk

Subject
Announcement
Reassurance
Option

Hello,

I'm away from my desk Oct. 10–21, 2007.

Your e-mail will be saved and read upon return.

If you have a pressing problem, please contact Susan Fryland at *susanfryland@vector.com*.

Regards,

Robert Grunman
Business Unit Manager
Vector, Inc.
robertgrunman@vector.com

 Tools

Pay as much attention to not answering your e-mail as you do to answering it

Nothing could be easier than writing an "I'm away from my desk" message, right? Wrong. These automatic messages often send inappropriate business signals. They get the message across, but not necessarily the one you want.

For example, the message "I'll be on vacation next week..." communicates unfavorable news. You're on vacation? Does this mean you're NOT working? When business has to be done 24-hours a day?

Even when you're taking the well-deserved break, it's a good idea not to brag about it. (Or even mention it. The worker who is still at his or her desk might not feel happy for you. They may be jealous, or even resentful.)

Avoid impersonal messages

"This e-mail will not be answered before March 19" is a clinker. It's clear that you're not at your desk, but the reader doesn't know why and may even wonder if you're coming back.

Such a bald statement of fact could even send a subtextual message of rejection. A colleague who has sent you an update on the status of a manufacturing proposal wants to be acknowledged and recognized, not find him or herself at the receiving end of an inhospitable message.

Worse yet, "This e-mail will not be answered before March 19" looks as if it's pretty clearly machine-generated. A colleague who takes the time to personally e-mail you information certainly doesn't want to be treated impersonally—there's way too much anonymity online already! Your colleague wants at least a phantom assurance that you're (tenuously) there, taking care of business, the same as always.

Personalize your away-from-my-desk message

The quickest way to humanize your "away from my desk" message is with a personal pronoun and, if possible, a vague reason. Try, for example, "I'll be traveling and unable to regularly respond to my e-mail Sept. 12–28." Note the use of the verb "I'll be unable to respond" instead of "I'll be unable to check."

The likelihood of a reply goes up if you're "checking" your mail; if you're going to dodge working at all, it's better to avoid misleading the reader and just tell him or her straight out that the chances are slim, indeed, that you're going to respond between such-and-such a date. Other options include "I'll be unable consult my e-mail between Feb. 13–30" or "I'm on leave from Jan. 6 to April 19."

Turn your away-from-my-desk message into an announcement of business success

Consider, as well, mentioning that you're away on a business-related trip when it's to your advantage. That way, you turn the "away from my desk" message into announcement of success. For example, "I'll be presenting Poetics 5.9 at the Pan-Pacific Innovative Technology Conference, August 8–15," tells the reader why you're gone, when you're gone, but also specifically why you're gone.

Explain, when you need to, that the entire office is closed

If the entire office is going to be closed for a specific reason, then take the time to explain the situation in your away-from-desk e-mail. "I will be unable to check e-mail May 7–9 during the move of our offices from 1523 North Clarendon to 223 North Broadway. If you need to contact me, please phone..."

Similarly, if the entire staff is taking time off for the holidays, then pass this information on to the readers. "On behalf of the Vector Sales Team, allow me to wish you a Happy Holiday Season. The Vector, Inc. Sales Office will resume regular working hours on Jan. 3, 2008."

Always include the exact days of your absence or the date of your return...give or take one or two days

Tagging on an extra day to your away-from-the-desk message may give you the time you need to catch up on your inbox. But remember to supply the readers with a specific date! The dates reassure the readers that their e-mail will be fielded and/or read. "I'll be back in the office on Dec. 12" is more reassuring than "I'll be back in the office next week."

Remember, as well, to include a sentence saying that either you'll read the e-mail upon your return or that someone else will. But don't leave the readers hanging. It may be perceived as rude. After all, they just sent you a message, presumably one you must read, should read, or would like to read. Therefore, you should always include information about what is going to happen to their e-mail and when it's going to be read.

Give the reader an option

In your absence, supply a colleague who the reader can contact, a phone number to call, or a way of reaching you directly in an emergency. This extra gesture shows that you care about your business relationships. Even if you're not at your desk when the e-mail arrives, the reader is acknowledged, informed, and taken care of.

Employee Transfer Request

Subject
Announcement

Accomplishments

Limitations

Incentive

Goodwill
Close

Jeanette,

I am writing to request a transfer from the Strategic Planning Team to the Strategic Implementation Team.

As you know, I have received very favorable performance reports for the last 4 reviews. Last year, I was proud to receive a Vector Employee Distinction for my work on the Poetics 5.9 Outsourcing. Under your supervision, I have helped develop plans that have enabled Vector, Inc. subsidiaries to grow by 7% in 5Q. I have, in fact, proven my abilities.

But for some time, I have felt as if I am not reaching my potential in my current position. I believe I am not contributing as much as I can. In addition, because of personality conflicts that have arisen within the SP team, I am less and less comfortable at my post.

Strategic Implementation, however, is suited for my career goals and path. It will allow me to make the most of my background in management and management training. For example, my 2-year experience with tolled information environments is of use as we shift gears toward tolling in the service sector. I believe that Philip Qun would welcome me aboard.

Let me know if you're open to further discussion.

Regards,

Sally Barb
Strategic Analyst
Vector Dimensional
sallybarb@vector.com

$\mathscr{T}$ools

Before you ask for the reader's help, recall all the good things you've done!

Readers are likely to be sympathetic to someone they owe a favor. But don't expect the reader to remember your good turns or your accomplishments. They won't. You have to put them on the table yourself. Once you've established your assets, you'll have the reader's attention so you can make your pitch.

Give the negatives without complaining

It's a truism that no one likes a complainer. This observation is particularly important in the context of business where complainers usually end up being isolated by the group and passed over for promotions.

All the more reason to use a factual tone when relaying negative information. Instead of saying the work situation in your department is so stressful that your esophagus burns all night long, simply observe that personality conflicts have arisen.

Make your goal seem inevitable

Argue your case so that your goal integrates into your history in such a way that the reader will perceive it as part of a seamless whole. In other words, make your goal seem logical, even destined. If you've done X in the past, and Y in the present, then, of course, you must do Z in the future. The reader will probably see that, too.

Remember to use specificity to persuade

Saying you're a valuable employee is one thing. Saying you've "enabled Vector Dimensional subsidiaries to grow by 7%" is another. When you're asking the boss for a change of assignment or a promotion, you have to furnish the reasons, and the more specific they are, the more convincing they'll be.

But set up the information properly! First make a targeted statement and then immediately follow it up with one or two examples. The general statement supplies context ("It will allow me to make the most of my background in management training"), while the specific application allows the reader to zoom in on compelling detail ("my 2-year experience with tolled information environments").

Options

For example...	Here's an illustration...
For instance...	Imagine...
Specifically...	Picture it like this...
Such as...	Think of it this way...
That means...	In other words...
In particular...	Explicitly...

Diagnose your writing problem

Imagine taking a snapshot of all the e-mail written in a firm on any given day.

Some employees write with ease, while those who write ineffective e-mails can easily be grouped in the following categories:

—problems beginning an e-mail

—problems figuring out what information should be included

—problems organizing the information

—problems structuring sentences

—problems in emotional tone

—problems stemming from bilingualism

—problems recognizing writing errors

—problems correcting writing errors

—problems in layout

These problems do not take years of writing therapy or instruction to correct. They require identifying the ineffective writing strategy and replacing it by a successful one.

Resignation

Subject
Announcement

Reason

Reassurance

Goodwill
Close

Laurence,

I have been offered the position as Chief Investment Analyst at Vector, Inc. After careful consideration, I decided to accept the post.

It was a difficult decision to make. During the last 2 years, I have worked hard to expand Lumina's real estate portfolio—I know you're aware of my accomplishments in that area. You also know that I have requested greater responsibility and flexibility in decision making. Vector, Inc. will provide me with the opportunities I seek.

Please know that I have enjoyed working with you, and hope to continue our business relationship in the future. In keeping with my contract, I will be at my post for one month from today (July 28, 2007). I am always available to do whatever I can to help you fill the position.

Sincerely,

Anne Seetel
Investment Analyst
Lumina Corp.
anneseetel@luminacorp.com

Tools

Resign right away

Decisiveness is a key trait in mid- and upper-level managers. Yet, at the moment of resignation, sometimes loyalties get in the way. It's difficult, after all, to tell someone you're abandoning ship, particularly if you've had a close, productive working relationship.

Potential emotional issues—either positive or negative—must be kept at bay. You want to maintain a professional tone in the resignation letter—friendly, but firm. After all, you might need a letter of reference from the reader in the future. Use your resignation to strengthen bridges, not break them. Try to leave the firm with as much style as when you came in.

Give a reason for the resignation

Although some workers may prefer a terse "This e-mail serves as notice of my resignation…," it's not always the best policy to pursue. This will only work if you've paved the way verbally. Otherwise, it hits a sour note. Provide a short, clear reason for your resignation that can circulate officially in the firm without drawing attention to the bad taste in your mouth.

Emphasize your goodwill

Telling your boss that you hope to remain in contact is a productive strategy. Because many business people move jobs every 3 or 4 years, it's possible that you and your boss might end up in the same office in another firm. All the more reason to include a positive observation about your work in the resignation letter. You don't have to overdo the praise, but a positive observation or two may also help your boss save face as the news of your resignation get passed around.

Netiquette

The semicolon hasn't fared very well in e-mail. And it used to be such a clever way of insisting on writing know-how and expertise! It had a heyday in the 19th century when English language sentences were long and complex. As the basic sentence unit shortened over the course of the last century, the need for the semicolon diminished. Once e-mail took over most of our communication needs, the semicolon lost more ground to the multitasking dash.

The main use of the semicolon in e-mail is to close long units in a list. When the components of the list require internal commas, then you use semicolons to separate one component in the list from the next. For example: "I worked hard to: increase subscription, particularly in the Asian market, prior to the IPO; restructure the bad debt caused by manufacturing shortfall in silicon output ITS; and managed the cross-functional Silicon Output R&D and Sales teams.

The other common service of the semicolon is less practical, more stylistic. It is called upon to unite two sentences that are closely linked in meaning, particularly when the writer wants to send a signal of formality. Like syntactic solder, the semicolon joins units without blending them together into a seamless whole. Its job is to maintain a boundary that connects; but also separates.

The semicolon does this job best when the two sentence components to be joined have more or less the same syntactic form. Consider the following example: "You state your regret simply; you don't dwell on it." The parallel structure in the sentences—their syntactic consistency—reinforces the close relationship between them. The semicolon tells the reader that the idea in the first unit is mirrored in the second.

Using a semicolon properly sends the message that you've mastered a professional mark of punctuation. Using it improperly, however, sends the message that you're not sure of your writing. Misuse suggests to the reader that there will be other mistakes as well—in the writing, of course—but also perhaps on the job.

Every writer is different

Every writer brings different strengths and weakness to a writing task. These writing strengths and weaknesses emerge from background factors, such as your interests, reading, and education. Even your taste in music, the places you've lived and traveled in, and the languages you've heard and speak all influence how you write. These differences in background result in different nuances in writing styles.

But they do not result in radically different business e-mails. An e-mail giving an approval for a particular course of action is more or less the same, no matter who writes it.

Problem in the Office

Subject Announcement

John, Jim

I would like to bring to your attention that the remodeling of the executive MIS offices is causing considerable disruption to the Finance Department.

Situation

We are under deadlines to finish working capital ratios as Q4 draws to a close. This task is all the more challenging in the wake of the Solaris merger. Both expectations and tensions are high.

Complication

Consequently, the power outages in the MIS wing have caused considerable disruption to the staff. Despite temporary insulation, the noise has reached noxious levels. Worker sick days are on the rise just when we need every desk filled.

Solution

I suggest that we temporarily move our offices to the Brooklyn branch until the remodeling work is completed. Another, more cost-effective option involves slotting the remodeling work in evening and night shifts.

Goodwill Close

I would be happy to discuss any solutions you might have.

Regards,

Bernadette Mason
Finance Manager
Vector, Inc.
bernadettemason@vector.com

$\mathcal{T}$ools

Tell the boss what he or she needs to know

Most upper level managers have their eyes on the big picture—details may be lost in the cracks. Never assume, therefore, that the boss is apprised of the trials and tribulations that you face on-the-job. Don't assume it's of interest, either.

Most of the time, you fix the problem yourself if you have the power to do so. Then you simply announce your accomplishment to colleagues and try to bring it to the attention of the higher-ups.

But when the issue touches upon you and your team, and you don't have the necessary authority to resolve it on your own, you need to make the issue known. If your complaint is a legitimate one, upper management will be grateful.

Indicate the number of employees affected and how the issue impacts their work

A complaint from one or two people is not high priority; a complaint that affects several—or even a lot—of workers needs attention. A complaint that can potentially lead to lawsuits is a complaint that needs to be settled right away.

If you can include evidence suggesting that the employees' ability to do their work is being compromised, you will probably score points with management, and solve the problem along the way.

Suggest how to fix the problem

The boss has the authority and you have the idea—it's a perfect match. But be careful! You don't want to tell the boss what to do—you just want to offer one or more workable options. That way, you've saved the boss's time and energy. He or she might research other solutions. Or maybe just make a decision based on your evidence.

Watch your tone

You know how complainers seem to whine? That tone can come across in an e-mail through word choices and sentence rhythm. And it's deadly. Business is about a lot of things—decisiveness, determination, creativity, and problem-solving. It's not about whining. For that reason, use neutral and factual language. A task should be "challenging," but not "impossible." Noise should be "noxious" but not "horrible."

Options

Would you consider...

I would like to bring to your attention...

Are you aware that...

What do you think about...

You're probably aware...

Have you had time to give consideration to...

Have you had a chance...

Did you happen to have time to...

Your viewpoint will be much appreciated regarding...

There's a situation that perhaps needs your attention...

Could you give me your opinion on...

It would help me to have your feedback on...

I would like to draw on your experience regarding...

You know better than I do how...

Allow me to make a suggestion...

Please allow me to describe...

Imitation is not copying

When you imitate a golf stroke, you adapt aspects of the stroke to your body and athletic skill. You cannot copy it exactly.

When you imitate a good writer, you use his or her document as a guideline, and adapt it to your purpose, context, and style. You do not copy it exactly.

Thank You for the Bonus

Li Ahn,

Subject
Announcement

I wanted to let you know right away that I appreciate the generous bonus.

Dedication

I've worked hard to obtain results for Vector in Accounts Receivable. Getting this job done has been and will continue to be my priority. I am happy that the wealth I've generated for the firm has been recognized and rewarded.

Gratitude

Thank you,

Si Petham
Account Analyst
Vector, Inc.
sipetham@vector.com

Tools

Reply rapidly to underscore sincerity

The sooner you thank the reader for a bonus, the more sincere you're perceived to be. A prompt thank you shows the reader that acknowledging the bonus takes precedence over other matters. It sends the signal of appreciation.

But tardiness in replying sends a different message. Yes, of course, you were too busy—everyone knows that already. But because we're all busy, we also all know that you can, in fact, find the five minutes you need to show your appreciation. The more you wait, the more perfunctory your thanks becomes. In other words, the longer an acknowledgement takes in a time-obsessed culture, the more its arrival is compromised.

Don't think that a quick, spoken thanks will suffice

Tapping your boss's elbow just before the meeting starts and thanking him or her for the bonus can't hurt, but it's not as effective—or as meaningful—as a written note. The difference between a spoken thank you and a written one is the difference between two language systems—one comes out of your mouth and usually doesn't leave a trace, the other hangs around for as long as the data lasts.

Written messages literally carry more weight in the Anglophone world than spoken messages. They have mass, substance, presence. Writing is tangible, durable, and resilient. This is the reason why writing has had legal force since its inception in Mesopotamia thousands of years ago. As soon as you have writing, you have proof. And when it comes to a thank you, proof of appreciation will have more impact than any quickly mumbled "thank you" will ever have.

Use the thank you to reinforce positive messages

The idea here is to avoid sounding like you're only acting in your own self-interest—even if, in the end, that's true! You want to take advantage of the thank-you-note moment to say something positive about the work for which you're being rewarded. After all, a thank you gets the boss's attention—use that momentum to your own advantage.

Include no more than one or two sentences referring to the work that you did—not in a bragging way, but in a sincere, straightforward way. Emphasize your commitment, your satisfaction, your pride in your success. That way you'll also be sending the message that you're a solid team player who can be counted on to perform.

Don't overdo it

Too much thanking, too much gratefulness, too much appreciation, and you look desperate or groveling. Too many explanation points, and you look juvenile. Too much tooting of the company horn, and you look like you're brown-nosing.

Keep it short, crisp, direct, and sincere. If each sentence is doing its job, there's no reason to keep going on and on. Here, as elsewhere, "less in more."

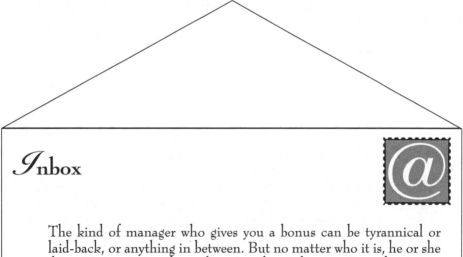

$\mathcal{I}$nbox

The kind of manager who gives you a bonus can be tyrannical or laid-back, or anything in between. But no matter who it is, he or she deserves recognition for making your bonus happen (even if someone else pressured them into doing it). A quick thank you may mean more to the tyrant than you'll ever know. It will reinforce good working relationships that exist and gently insist on the potential where they don't.

But even more importantly, the courtesy of a thank you supplies proof of social graces. And in many firms, your ability to act correctly, politely, and with dignify is synonymous with self-confidence.

*E*dit

Before: complimenting the mentor

Dear Ms. Dillon,

Please allow me to take this opportunity to hereby convey and express my heartfelt gratitude for the insightful observations that you generously offered on the occasion of the Human Resources meeting at Vector, Inc., headquarters on August 12, 2007.

In point of fact, yesterday's meeting, as you obviously know, had taken an unfortunate turn during the sustained discussions of the proposed viability and necessity of the Byron hires. Understandably, I was neither pleased, nor happy, nor hopeful, at the prospect of convincing the Compensation Analysts with the strength, logic, and rationale of my data, despite all the extensive and thorough preparation that I personally undertook prior to the meeting to make my case as clear and comprehensible as possible and despite the overwhelming amount of evidence at my disposal.

The well-chosen timing of your cogent remarks and the evident force with which you delivered them not only secured the Analysts' considerable attention, it also allowed them to reassess, reconsider, and reevaluate their position in light of the fact of your sharp observations. It was at that very moment that the tables turned, so to speak, and my case was given its due, thanks to you.

Please let me say here once more how valuable your support was to the likelihood and achievability of the hires. And the success to which you contributed is not to be forgotten.

I remain at your disposal,

Lisa Harding
MIS Assistant Manager
Vector, Inc.
lisaharding@vector.inc

The problem

Tone! You don't want to sound like you're from the old country, as though you just got off the boat. Traditional and conservative language is one thing, old-fashioned and outmoded language another. If you have to "hereby" anything nowadays, it's probably a summons to appear in court! Arcane language still plays in legal documents, but outside of this context, it risks comic effect. Business e-mail wants to transact information from the reader to the writer—it doesn't want to put on airs, adopt literary affects, or show how smart the writer is. Most lofty vocabulary is also to be avoided for the same reasons. It runs a risk of alienating the reader or just sending the message that the writer is out of touch with the real world. "Insightful" and "cogent" have their place in literature or even special business docs, but it's hard to make a case for them in a short, everyday business e-mail.

Redundancy! Phrases such as "in point of fact" and "in light of the fact that" just waste time and space. They also make the writing tiresome. Writers who are trying too hard to be clear often end up being redundant. Instead of making the idea sharper, all those extra words block the view. Because redundancy comes in many forms, it's often difficult to catch at first. One of the easiest patterns to identify is the "doublet" and "triplet," such as "convey and express" and "reassess, reconsider, and re-evaluate." In a business e-mail, one verb will do, thank you very much.

Brown-nosing! When sweet-talk turns obsequious, and flattery is borderline adulation, you're not convincing anybody. Most bosses like to be respected, but few of them really want their employees to grovel. Overdoing your thanks, your praise, or your gratitude will probably work against you. It might embarrass the reader, or worse yet, raise questions about your motivation. It might even make the boss suspicious. Someone who overdoes the flattery is usually trying to get something.

The solution

Use up-to-date language. If upper management uses the word, if you hear it on the business report or read it in the business section of the paper, you can be pretty sure that the same word should be in your vocabulary, too. But if your grandma says it, if you picked it up in an historical novel, or saw it in a contract, chances are high that it's not the right word for the job. For example, being at someone's "disposal" or having facts at your "disposal" might have worked last century, but nowadays the word conjures up trash, as in "trash disposal" or "garbage disposal."

Remember that redundancy weakens your writing. Redundancy sends the wrong signals—that you're not paying attention to the writing, that you don't know when your point is clear, and that you don't realize you're wasting time—your own and the reader's. The latter is the most serious crime.

If you edit an e-mail for concision and get rid of all the redundancy, often its length will be halved and sometimes even quartered. If you apply that ratio to all the e-mail in your inbox, you have some idea of what's at stake. Words are taking up space on our chips, in our hard drive, on our screen—but they're often not functioning.

"The extensive and thorough preparation that I personally undertook prior to the meeting" is really just "I was prepared for the meeting." "In point of fact" should just be "in fact" and "in light of the fact that" should be "in light of." And so on.

Make your compliments sincere. If somebody has done you a favor, a straightforward thanks is in order. Just by specifically saying what the person did and offering your gratitude is enough.

After: complimenting the mentor

Nikki,

I just want to quickly thank you for lending me your support in the HR Policy Meeting yesterday.

The Compensation Analysts were so against the necessity of the Byron hires that they weren't listening to the facts—I don't even think they reviewed the stats I prepared. Although I pride myself on my communication skills, I was becoming frustrated. You stepped in at just the right moment. By voicing your support, you enhanced my creditability. And we got the hires.

Thanks again,

Lisa Harding
MIS Assistant Manager
Vector, Inc.
lisaharding@vector.com

CHAPTER EIGHT

Leadership

INCLUDING

Request for Cooperation

Handling Rumors

Correcting a Colleague

Reprimanding a Subordinate

Reference

Motivating an Employee

171

Request for Cooperation

Subject
Announcement

Situation

Strategy

Goodwill
Close

Jean, Michelle, Chris, Lo,

Upper management has brought to my attention that the M5 account has capital expenditures inconsistent with allocated assets recorded in the Q2 budget.

Because you are all valued employees, it is assumed that you had very good reasons for signing off on the budget. These inconsistencies, however, reflect poorly on our projections and compromise our performance as a team. They must be rectified immediately.

Please send me information on the net present value, internal rate of return, and payback period of Lumina Corp. by the close of the business day, Tuesday, March 10. Once GIGO is ruled out, I'm certain you will have a legitimate explanation for the discrepancy.

Bring the necessary docs to Friday's staff meeting and feel free to contact me with your concerns.

Regards,

Sheila Tann
Investment Officer
Vector, Inc.
sheilatann@vector.com

*T*ools

Consider dropping the "I" pronoun to promote collective authority

While me-and-you pronoun usage is usually a default setting in business e-mail, situations exist where you don't want to make your "I" vulnerable. The "I" is always happy to congratulate workers on results, but this same "I" might be less than enthusiastic about confronting workers regarding fiscal discrepancies.

In censoring the "I," you lessen your personal involvement. For example, "It has become apparent that" emphasizes the unarguable facts of a situation, while "Upper Management has brought to my attention..." puts the onus on the entire management structure. You're not the one making the request; they are.

Keep the tone direct and upbeat

When you're trying to get someone to do something, it's much better to foster confidence instead of resistance. Avoid accusations and insults until you have all the facts. Toward that end, include phrases or sentences in your request affirming the employees' value to the firm and/or expressing the likelihood that the situation will be easily resolved. Show you have confidence in your reports—you'll earn loyalty for it. And until the truth comes out, they're probably worth it.

Specify exactly what you need

If you don't name it, you won't get it. Be sure to specify exactly what information you need, when you need it by, and what the result will be.

Writing skills cut to the bottom line

Employers know that poor writing ability in the workforce compromises productivity and impacts results. Any person who has to read and reread the same e-mail in order to understand it usually gets annoyed. Time spent trying to decipher an e-mail is time that should have been spent on other tasks.

*N*etiquette

Writers make mistakes when they push the "send" button. It happens to us all—once. We want to mail a complaint to colleague, and it ends up going to an entire mailing list! Writers are particularly liable to making this error when they're angry, when they've written an e-mail they probably shouldn't send, or even one that they *know* they don't want to send. But they do anyway. By accident.

Because everyone does it, readers tend to be generous the first time. They'll probably read the e-mail they shouldn't have received, of course—gossip will follow, if it's gossip-worthy. But whatever bad publicity you generate will likely blow over, provided the revelations contained in your e-mail aren't beyond the pale. It's often better, in these cases, not to send an apology, which will just draw more attention to the matter instead of helping it die down. The reader who would have deleted the message as spam might take a sudden interest.

But if you make this kind of mistake frequently, or regularly, you're sending a signal that you're disorganized, or inattentive, or under so much stress that you're unable to do your job properly. You may even raise the suggestion that you're in poor mental health! Systematic mistakes are worrisome; occasional ones usually aren't.

To protect yourself from mailing mishaps, it's better not to write anything in an e-mail that you wouldn't want to share with colleagues. E-mail should always be written with full awareness that you really can't ever control where the information goes and that your e-mails might be forwarded without your knowledge. Or there may be blind readers on the copy who you know nothing about.

Many firms have proprietary e-mail policies in which each employee's mail is considered their business property. E-mail monitoring, therefore, might be company policy. The employee's consent or knowledge may not even be necessary. Monitoring might be sporadic or continual. For these reasons, it's always better to exercise extreme caution when e-mailing about a sensitive subject. Especially when you're angry.

Handling Rumors

FOR YOUR EYES ONLY

Donna, Fred, Maryanne,

Subject Announcement

Rumors are circulating regarding violation of Child Labor Laws in the manufacture of Vector, Inc., products.

Rumor

Specifically, the Vortex quartzite mouse accessory launched in January 2007 is under fire for allegedly employing under-age miners in the extraction fields of Upper Egypt. The recent mining tragedy in that country brought the mines into the spotlight and Vector along with it. If some of the children who perished in the recent disaster prove to be Vector employees, we will have a full-blown scandal on our hands.

Analysis

At present, I am unable to say with certainty if any of the allegations are substantive or not. Vector is investigating the situation. As you know, Vector does not support or condone any violation of Child Labor Laws. In the unlikely case that any of the allegations prove true, we will, of course, do our best to make amends for any errors on our part.

Response

Kris will be setting up a conference call tomorrow morning to discuss a game plan. In the meantime, please assure your colleagues and reports that: (1) Vector has, at present, no knowledge of any violations of Child Labor Laws; (2) Vector has a record of compliance with the Child Protection Act; and (3) Vector is doing everything in its power to get to the bottom of the story.

Goodwill Close

I know I can count on you.

Deborah Larkin
Operation Manager
Vector, Inc.
deborahlarkin@vector.com

$\mathcal{T}$ools

Warn employees about bad news in a face-to-face meeting or with a phone call

People like to hear bad news first before they read it. In a face-to-face or videoconference, voice and body language provide reassurance or reveal a disconnect between what is being said and how the speaker feels about it. On the phone, the listener concentrates on voice clues. But in an e-mail, words have to do all the work.

However, writing has a great deal of authority in Anglophone cultures. An e-mail often seems more truthful than a rumor heard at the water cooler. If you tell me over the phone that a problem is looming large, I'll believe you. But if you send me an e-mail about it, I'll not only believe you, I'll have to do something about it.

Use confidentiality markers when you need to

"For Your Eyes Only," "Confidential," and "Nondisclosure Policies Apply" remind the reader that he or she is being taken into confidence with sensitive information. But passwords and biometric coding are not a cure-all. You are always relying on the employee's discretion.

If you know and trust your team, confidentiality probably isn't a big issue. But always be aware that a disgruntled employee might seize upon the chance to break the news to the press or share the disclosure with your competitors. For that reason, once again, be very careful with sensitive information. Be discrete with what you write in an e-mail and be careful where you send it.

Get right to the point with unpleasant news

A confident boss immediately lays out the problem; a worried, insecure one will stall. Putting off bad news doesn't make it easier—avoidance makes the confrontation worse. For these reasons, state your bad news straight out, in a clear, direct, no-nonsense tone. The worst is already over.

Stick to the facts

In a potential crisis situation, everyone appreciates a level head. Objectivity provides a remedy. Let the facts speak for themselves. Don't speculate, don't interpret, don't comment, and don't apologize. That way, you can't be criticized for relaying misleading information—you confined yourself to the facts as you know them.

Give special attention to the goodwill close

In a factual e-mail announcing bad news, the one place where you can emphasize emotion is in the close. Reinforce your determination to triumph, your belief in the team, or your confidence that the situation will be brought rapidly under control. A personalized note at the end can help put the bad news in perspective. Make certain that your close carries emotional buoyancy by starting your sentence with "I."

Options

I know I can count on you...   I know I can rely on you...

I know I can depend on you...   I know I can put my trust in you...

I glad you're with me on this...   I know that we can solve this...

I know we're going to get through this...

I know when we put our heads together, we'll figure it out...

Now more than ever, I'm reassured to have you aboard...

I have every confidence that we can handle this crisis together...

I know I'm working with the best possible team at this difficult time...

I'm confident that together we can handle the situation...

Writing errors fall into patterns

Recognize the pattern of your mistakes. Figuring out the pattern to your errors is the first step toward correcting it. Perhaps you use the word "being" a lot in your e-mail. "Being" is a word that usually leads to poor, if not convoluted, sentence structure. Looking for the word "being" and removing it from your e-mail forces you to rethink sentence structure. Better sentence structure leads to greater clarity and increased reading pleasure.

Correcting a Colleague

	Jeb,
Subject Announcement	I am concerned that I am not communicating as clearly as I need to.
Situation	I have just learned of a press release that included results of benchmarking efforts against Veranda. The link to the test suit mentioned in the press release violates exactly what the agreement intends to restrict (please see highlighted section attached).
Problem	In the March 3 note that I sent you on this subject, I tried to make it clear that the agreement does not permit publication of the benchmarking results. Instead of disclosing the data, I suggested that the customers/press judge for themselves.
Reminder	If you were still determined to use the benchmarking data after our last communication, I would have hoped you involved me. I volunteered to help you, and so did others on my team.
Teamwork	Now my chief concern is going forward. I am highly motivated to succeed. I want to be part of a team dedicated and determined to win in the marketplace. I hope that my value is in assisting others to find ways to meet business objectives.
Moving Forward	As we move on, I hope you will allow me to show you that it is to your advantage to involve me in these kinds of matters.
	Amelie Forsthyme IGF and Corporate Operations Vector, Inc. *amelieforsthyme@vector.com*

Tools

Be careful when correcting colleagues who are not your direct reports

One of the most difficult problems for a worker to encounter in a firm is having to make a request from someone who is not a direct report. When push comes to shove, they don't have to do what you say...do they?

To increase the likelihood that these colleagues will, in fact, follow your advice, you have to persuade them of your authority. They also have to feel that the suggestions you're making have their interests, rather than just yours, in mind.

Cite your own error before citing the reader's

Admitting you're not perfect, that you make errors, often causes the reader to feel less threatened (or even sympathetic). You know you're not always 100 percent; you make mistakes, too. Instead of looking down on your reader, you look eye-to-eye.

Ironically, this strategy can end up increasing your ability to persuade, rather than diminishing it, particularly with a reader who doesn't want to be told what to do, who is jealous, or who is defensive. At the very least, an expression of self-doubt gets the reader's attention.

Don't dwell on the reader's mistake

Summarize the mistake quickly and efficiently, even when you see the ramifications multiplying in your mind's eye. Vent privately, but not in the e-mail. If the reader feels threatened, he or she will retreat just at the point when you most need to win cooperation. You have to point out the error to correct it, but you don't have to rub the reader's face in it.

Cover yourself

If you warned the reader that a particular line of action was ill advised, remind him or her that you saw this problem coming. It may help cultivate trust. And in the event that documents regarding the incident circulate in the firm, you will reassert your I-told-you-so each time the document is read.

Concentrate on the future

Once the damage is done, it's done—a strong leader doesn't mourn, shame others, or show remorse. Instead he or she consolidates the base and plans for further action. It is just at this point when it's effective to reiterate company values. Tell the reader you're competitive, dedicated to winning, and so on. Offer your continued willingness to help.

By focusing on your own strengths instead of the reader's weaknesses, you shift the discussion away from blame for past events toward proactive teamwork in the present and in the future. Your goodwill might not be enough to secure an ideal working relationship, but it's a step in the right direction.

*N*etiquette

Just because you wrote your e-mail promptly doesn't mean you'll get a response promptly. We tend to think we should, though. The speed with which e-mail is written and delivered seems to suggest that we shouldn't have to wait. But we often do.

Readers don't necessary read upon the writer's demand. There may be very good reasons for this—deadlines for a project that take precedence, unforeseen developments that require immediate attention, involvement in meetings that preclude e-mail interaction, or the decision to not reply.

Without exact information, a delay in reply is difficult to judge. Are you on the backburner or just on temporary hold? Is a nonreply the only reply you're going to get? Did your document get waylaid in cyberspace or by your correspondent? Or did your correspondent just forget?

The only way to avoid anxiety in this situation is to remind yourself that you sometimes delay in replying, too. It happens to us all, for the reasons discussed above. But if the delay in replying becomes pronounced, it's perfectly appropriate to send your e-mail again with a "Second Send" announcement in the subject line.

Choosing the exact moment to send the reminder takes judgment. It depends on your relationship with the correspondent—senior managers get more time than junior managers, for example. It also depends on the urgency of the e-mail—if it doesn't require immediate action, the reminder can probably wait. And it depends on the disposition of the correspondent—someone who is usually prompt will understand if you get back to him or her relatively soon, asking about a reply. Once you've weighted all the factors, send the reminder. If you still don't get a response, then pick up the phone.

Reprimanding a Subordinate

Subject Announcement

Past Performance Problems

Current Performance Problems

Correction

Looming Dismissal

Melanie,

News of your poor performance has once again reached my office.

You will recall that your direct supervisor Steve Homes and I spoke with you two weeks ago regarding misreporting in financial projections traced to inaccuracies in your accounts. At that meeting, you volunteered—as I noted in an e-mail to you on May 6—that you were facing personal problems. You assured us that you were going to resolve the issues and that your performance would return to the high level that Vector expects.

Steve has just informed me that you arrived at the Vector HQ yesterday in poor health. Before you left the Finance Office, you promised to finish your work—already two days behind schedule—at home. Instead of following through, you phoned in later in the day to say that it was impossible for you to complete the assignment.

While Vector fosters a company spirit in which workers are always ready to pitch-in to help each other, you are increasingly exhibiting a pattern in which you expect others to systematically fill in for you. This behavior is not tolerated.

If your job performance does not improve, you will face a suspension—even dismissal. Both Steve and I regret this situation, but your behavior has left us with no alternative.

Regards,

Tem Burns
Director of Finance
Vector, Inc.
temburns@vector.com

Tools

Try dropping the personal pronoun in a negative e-mail

Instead of saying, "I have learned," try "It has come to my attention." By shifting the burden of responsibility from the "I" pronoun to the impersonal "it," you emphasize that the criticism is coming from an impersonal, impartial source. You are just the spokesperson. There's no need to get angry with you because you're just the messenger.

Put facts first in a negative e-mail

Authority derives, in part, from knowing the facts—and communicating them logically, clearly, and objectively. Before criticizing the team or an employee, gather as many facts as you can—the more specific, the better—dates, times, and numbers. Be as precise and accurate as possible.

Evidence is difficult to dispute, particularly when there's a mass of it. Although vague accusations can be neutralized with a quick explanation, a mass of evidence requires careful refutation. When facts are laid out one after another, a point-by-point refutation is required. Most employees won't attempt one, particularly when the accusations are coming from more than one authority. In short, if your facts are verifiable, they probably won't be disputed.

State the warning clearly

The risks have to be clearly articulated using cause-and-effect. If you do X, we'll do Y. If you violate these policies, we can fire you.

Put the ball back in the reader's court in the close

Offer to explain to the reader anything in company policy that's unclear. Then assign responsibility to the reader for clarifying any information that needs to be clarified. Finally, indicate that if you do not hear from the reader about the need for clarification, then it is understood by both parties that the policies are clear.

> ### Identify the best
>
> Put copies of the best e-mails you receive in a *style file* to consult for future use.
>
> Put copies of the worst e-mails you receive in a *disaster file* to learn what to avoid.

*A*dvice

You want the boss to be a boss. That means someone you can respect for their greater understanding, insight, and experience with the issues. You want this person to be clear, direct, and fair. You don't want to be dealt with tyrannically, nor do you want to feel that you've got too much leeway or that you're mostly on your own. You want guidance when you need it. You want to feel as if the boss is protecting and fighting for you. The boss should be loyal to you...at least most of the time. And you'll give your loyalty, as well as your best work, in return.

The boss can impart authority in an e-mail in several ways. First of all, through tone—that means, in part, choosing a vocabulary that is slightly elevated, but not lofty. For example, "difficulty," "problem," "obstacle," and "hurtle" all sound like a boss, but "screw up," "mess," or "nightmare" don't.

Straightforward declarative sentences also send an authoritative signal. Compare "Team members who cannot comply with security policies will be dismissed" with "In addition, and further to this situation, it is my personal duty to clearly and precisely inform you again for the second time in the last 6 months that any of our employees who is not following and obeying company rules, guidelines, and regulations will be most certainly reported for severe disciplinary action as promptly as possible." The first sentence is clear and confident. The second one tries to borrow the language of authority and ends up looking defensive and unsure. Similarly, run-on sentences and stream-of-consciousness sentences undermine authority.

The paragraphs the boss writes should also be orderly and reflect control of language and analytical thought. The main point should be immediately clear, not buried in the middle of a longish paragraph or left up to grabs. The quickest way of maintaining authority through paragraph structure is to keep sentences short and order them logically. The first sentence of each paragraph should announce the focus of paragraph content.

An e-mail that emphasizes objectivity and impartiality, even when its message is negative or threatening, sends the signal that the boss is in control. There is no need for the boss to blame the reader, to make the reader feel guilty, to insult the reader, or to flame the reader. Inappropriate responses call your confidence into question. If you spell out your news, even your bad news, in a confident, straightforward way, you'll get the respect you deserve.

*N*etiquette

Knowing the difference between a dash and a hyphen separates the pros from the amateurs. A dash (—) is long; a hyphen is short (-). They're as different as software is from hardware. Look at it this way: The dash is bigger. It has to do with big things, such as parts of a sentence. You can use it to append information, insert an aside, or for dramatic effect. The dash creates a vigorous pause between closely related components.

You promised to finish your work—already two days behind schedule—at home.

You will face suspension—even dismissal.

The hyphen is smaller. It has to do with little things, such as little words. It's mostly used between adjectives and sometimes nouns.

The boss gave him the brush-off last night at the baseball game.

That is a fail-safe system designed just for your company.

The hyphen suggests that the two words are possibly on their way to becoming one. "Semicolon," for example, used to be spelled, "semi-colon." Whether hyphenated words lose their hyphen and meld into a single unit depends on a complex of factors governing language evolution as a whole.

Using the dash and hyphen properly sends the signal that you're in control of your writing. And if you know how to write, your managers will probably think that you're pretty good at other things, too.

Friends don't let friends write badly

Some of writers I've worked with—writers who had very poor written communication skills to begin with—sometimes go on to help other workers on their staff. Mentoring in the workplace includes tips about sentence length.

Reference

Ms. Schaftner,

Subject Announcement

As the Director of Media Analysis at Vector Dimensional, I would like to recommend without reservation my former Senior Analyst, Chris Deibs, for the position of Assistant Director of Media Relations at Height Corp.

Narrative 1

Chris was already on board at Vector when I became Director of Media Analysis in 2005. For the first year, Chris was among my indirect reports, but he quickly distinguished himself by initiating the Vector Tracking Project. I must admit that when I heard of Chris' proposal, I was not quick to see its worth—that is until Chris requested an appointment with me, outlined the disadvantages of our search engines and provided a clear-headed strategy for correction.

Narrative 2

Due in part to the success of the Tracking Project, Chris was promoted to Senior Analyst and was my direct report for the next 14 months. During that time, he recognized and culled a reference pattern based on emotional response that is now a part of our Standard Search Returns.

Description

In the performance of his duties, Chris has never disappointed. Because he likes a challenge, he has consistently met, and often surpassed, expectations. He is respected by his subordinates and superiors alike, and is generally possessed of a congeniality that makes teams thrive. He inspires loyalty and pushes others to achieve more than they would have thought possible. I recommend him without hesitation.

Goodwill Close

Please give me a call if you'd like to discuss his qualification in detail.

Sincerely,

Dick Ballen
Director of Media Analysis
Vector Dimensional
dickballen@vector.com

$\mathscr{T}$ools

Follow the conventions of the recommendation

The recommendation includes: information about the writer's position; how the writer knows the employee and for how long; narrates the employee's accomplishments; describes the employee's people skills; and predicts continued success for the employee.

Use sequential narrative when conveying an employee's record

Narrative has to do with the order in which information is laid out. The most common narratives are sequential, and relay information in strict chronological order.

In a recommendation, narratives usually begin at the point when the writer met the employee and end in the present. Narratives are usually easy to write, provided that the writer doesn't violate chronological order—which leads to a bunch of problems.

Divide the narrative into sections

One big narrative paragraph isn't as effective as two or three smaller paragraphs with good lead sentences. But it's often difficult to figure out where to break the paragraphs up—after all, chronology just keeps going!

Sometimes the break between paragraphs can be arbitrary, in the sense that the first narrative paragraph focuses on accomplishments in 2004 and the second on 2005. Change of year, change of paragraph. This structuring device is easy to use.

A more sophisticated technique involves identifying a promotion, a commendation or a noteworthy result, and using that as a watershed to lead into a new paragraph. When you structure the narrative according to accomplishments—instead of arbitrary time markers—they really shine.

Include a paragraph of character description

Prospective employers want to know how their potential hire will fit in on the new team. What kind of people skills does he or she have? What kind of person is he or she? Assign one or two points per sentence, drawing attention to the most relevant traits for the position.

Be careful with vocabulary

Saying someone is a go-getter will probably work, but saying the same person is an active self-starter and problem-solver is probably too much. The temptation here is to fall back on buzzwords. A couple are okay, but use too many and the recommendation looks as if it's been generated more by a machine than a supervisor. Buzzwords show that you're up-to-date; you just don't want to overdo.

Options

I'd like to recommend...

I highly recommend...

I am pleased to recommend...

I recommend without hesitation...

I am happy to recommend...

I am delighted to recommend...

I have had the privilege of working with...

It is with great pleasure that I recommend...

I have had the opportunity to collaborate...

I have had the pleasure of knowing _____ for ___ years...

I have had the pleasure of working with _____ for ___ years...

_____ has always struck me as the kind of person who would go far...

Poorly written e-mail leads to more e-mail

A muddled e-mail requires clarification. It requires yet another e-mail.

Motivating an Employee

Carlos,

Subject
Announcement

I hope you weren't serious when you suggested that I take you off the Poetics 5.9 account!

Confidence

Look: We knew from the get-go that Poetics 5.9 would be a hard sell in the current market. That's why I put you on the account, and why you accepted—you've excelled in similar circumstances before. You knew when you took the post what you were up against. And you knew *there was no one else who I would trust—then or now*.

Comparison

Remember last year, right about this time, when we were at rock bottom with Ode 2.4? Then the state market broke wide open and we scored BIG. But it wouldn't have happened if we hadn't prepared the terrain.

Advice

The recent setbacks have hit us all hard, but that's just it— they're setbacks, NOT a death sentence. It may look like we're at saturation, but the stats says it's maturity. The virtual office trend is in our favor, but we're too early in the curve for the margin.

We have to be patient.

Goodwill
Close

I need your help on this one, Carlos. I'll give you a call in the coming days, and we'll talk it through.

Regards,

Florence Williams
Chief Sales Manager
Vector, Inc.
florencewilliams@vector.com

Tools

Remember that a little reassurance goes a long way

No matter what our job is, we've all had the feeling that we just can't do it. Then someone comes along and says, but you can! And we do.

A good motivator knows how to bring out the best in his or her reports. And one of the simplest ways of enabling an employee is by expressing confidence in his or her know-how, skills, and ability to triumph. Sometimes when employees express doubt about their ability to do something, they're really just asking for reassurance.

Make a comparison to a difficult situation that ended up being a total success

Often when we're worried about a potential outcome, we think of other situations that ended in failure—and we skip over other situations that ended in success. A suitable comparison to a difficult situation that ended up okay brings the message home that difficulty is often a prerequisite to success.

But choose your illustration carefully! If you compare the employee's present difficulties to the problems facing the Allied Forces during WWII, you may get a whimsical smile, but you won't necessarily bolster confidence. It's better to chose something from the employee's own experience, if you know enough about it to find a parallel.

If not, choose a situation from your own experience and begin the comparison with, "I think I know how you feel. When I was dealing with the Height Corp. account...." When you share your feelings with an employee, you strengthen personal bonds. You also model for him or her the realities of getting ahead—it's hard work and doubts are normal. We must be patient and carry on.

Become conscious of what you're doing

In order to improve your skills, you have to recognize your errors. As successful overachievers, many busy executives are already onto the next task instead of finalizing the one they just began. Sometimes just slowing down an e-mail and taking the time to reread it carefully can lead to insight.

*N*etiquette

E-mail has changed how writers express emphasis. In the old days, italics were king. If you needed to draw attention to a word, phrase, or idea, you just switched to italics and it was done. If for some reason the italics didn't work on your word processor, you used underlining. Italics and underlining "mean" the same thing: Pay attention! The change in style means I'm saying something important!

Then the first e-mail programs arrived and italics got clobbered. Some e-mail programs allowed the writer to see the italics in the message before sending, but when it arrived at the other end, it was gobbledygook. Because writing has to have emphasis—ways of showing the reader that some words need special attention—stopgap strategies emerged, such as framing the idea with underscores, as in _be patient_!

As e-mail programs improved, the stopgap method for italics became less common. At present, many e-mail programs allow you to send an e-mail with italics from one computer to another without compatibility problems. The use of italics among employees in a single company is usually not an issue because most workers will be using the same software and hardware.

But the emphasis issue doesn't end there. Another form of emphasis emerged during the italics' dark days—capitalization. While the busy business reader, skimming his or her way through a document, might not give italics their due, capitals always garner attention...provided they're not overdone. The trick with using capitals for emphasis has to do with restraint. Because a lot of capitals produce the effect of shouting, you don't want them to scream all over the screen. Instead of producing the desired effect, the capitals will cancel each other out.

Boldface type also emerged as a method of emphasis during the early days of e-mail. Most often, boldface type appears when writers are trying to contrast different kinds of emphasis, using capitals for one kind of idea, italics/underlining for another, and bold for the third.

So where does that leave you? First, remember that too much emphasis has a self-canceling effect; second, if the e-mail is casual, use capitalization for emphasis, provided that it doesn't begin to rant; third, use underlining and italics for more formal e-mails; fourth, use bold if you're contrasting with capitals; and five, use all of them (sparingly!) if the layout and content of the e-mail require that you segment the reader's attention to specific, important points in different ways.

*A*dvice

Up, down, or across the chain of command?

Think about it—you don't present yourself to the boss the same way you do a colleague or to a subordinate. Or at least, you shouldn't!

Different communication contexts elicit different communication styles. For example, you don't roll over in bed in the morning and speak to your partner the same way you'll speak to staff at the budget meeting later in the day. The vocabulary is different. The sentence structure is different. The presentation is different.

Your partner might hear, "Oh no! It'stimetogetupagain," complete with a curse word and a mumble. Your staff, however, will hear, "Good Morning! I want to thank you all for coming to this IT meeting on such short notice. First of all, we need to address...."

The same principle holds true in e-mail. Different readers require different vocabulary, sentence structure, and presentation. You may write to your boss, "I need to discuss a confidential HR issue with you. Could you make time to see me on Thursday?" Your colleagues might receive an e-mail like this: "Let's try and speak today about the current HR issue in the department. Are you free at noon?" Your subordinates would probably receive an e-mail more along the lines of: "Please meet in my office at 3 PM this afternoon to discuss the HR issue."

Differences in communication styles sometimes make writers nervous. After all, you're still the same person in different contexts, aren't you? Isn't all this code shifting sort of schizophrenic?

Yes, of course it is. But at the same time, it isn't. Language allows us to express different aspects of our personality. That's one of its great gifts— it's a marvelous, flexible tool. It's like a white shirt—you can wear it with a suit, with jeans, or open over your underwear. You're still the same person. What's changed is which aspects of your personality are emphasized.

With the boss, you usually want to call attention to the fact that you've got what it takes for a promotion, a raise, or a bonus. Therefore, you communicate that you have things under control, that you have your eyes on the big picture but haven't lost sight of the details, that you love a challenge, that no mountain is too big to climb, or that you're in a constant I-can-do-it mode.

Colleagues see a slightly different you—you could be an ally or a rival. With them, you want to emphasize that you're going to hold up your end of the bargain; that you won't let them down; that you won't backstab or undercut them when they're not looking; and that your success will complement, rather than detract from theirs.

Subordinates want to be assured that you're fair and that they can count on your authority—when they don't know what to do, you will (or you'll figure it out). You want to emphasize that you're aware when they're performing well and when they're not giving their all, that you can help them get ahead if they show you they deserve it, that their loyalty to you will pay off, and so on.

Differences in communication style reinforce the pecking order of the business hierarchy—who's at the top, who's in the middle, who's at the bottom. In e-mail, differences in communication requirements play out in a sliding scale with formality at one end and casualness at the other. Generally speaking, greater formality inheres with the boss and often with subordinates. E-mails to colleagues tend be a bit more informal.

But it's not cut-and-dry. It depends, to a large degree, on context. Here are some things to keep in mind:

First consider the corporate culture in your firm—if it's on the formal side, your e-mail should be, too. Are women allowed to wear open-toe shoes? Are men allowed to go without ties? Do workers have Casual Fridays? How casual is a Casual Friday? Also consider what kind of business the firm is in and how it conducts that business. Is it in the techno music industry or does it specialize in corporate mergers? Does it encourage camaraderie among employees with frequent social events? How does it portray itself in the community? Pay close attention to how upper-reaches of management dress and behave, because they often attained their positions in part by their ability to reflect the image of the firm.

Now consider the nature of the subject matter of the e-mail. Is a lot of money involved? Large sums tend to elicit a more formal e-mail style. Is the subject matter banal or is it considered an official document? Let acronyms and abbreviations into an e-mail about company picnic, but don't cut corners in an announcement of litigation—spell everything out, and use italics, not capitals, for emphasis. Would you rather reply over the phone than send your response over the net? How serious is the paper trail? Serious paper trail, serious tone.

Lastly, note the circumstances of the e-mail itself. Is it the first time you've received an e-mail on the subject? Or the 10th? Is your e-mail part of a complex chain of forwards and replies or is it a stand-alone? Are you forced to reply immediately or can you take your time? Is it a short e-mail or a long one? Is it introducing a situation or commenting on one? Long e-mail threads tend to favor abbreviated responses. Stand-alone e-mail usually strikes a more formal note, particularly when it has financial or legal content.

The best way of understanding the e-mail style that you should use is by observing the style in the ones you get. What tone does the boss use? Your colleagues? Your reports? Figure out who the best writers are in your firm and follow their clues.

Do...

Gauge the appropriate level of formality by considering the image of the firm, the reader, the subject matter, and the circumstances of the e-mail.

Use acronyms, abbreviations, and in-house slang in casual e-mails.

Drop the reader's name in the salutation if your e-mail is part of a back-and-forth, or the next installment in a long thread, or written to a close colleague.

Consider using one-word sentences and one-liners when appropriate.

Feel free to use sentence fragments, capitalization, and lots of dashes in casual e-mail.

Don't...

Make the mistake of thinking that all the e-mail you write should conform to the same style—it doesn't.

Use the markers of hardcopy, such as memo headers, in e-mail unless you're absolutely certain they're required by the firm.

Forget to write out contractions, acronyms, abbreviations, and most small numbers in formal e-mail.

Use incomplete sentences and one-word sentences in formal e-mail.

Choose capitalization for emphasis if the context is formal—use italics.

CHAPTER NINE

Deals and Contracts

INCLUDING

Summary of a Deal

Analysis of a Contract

Technical Concepts Explained

Advice on Compliance

Changes in a Draft

Summary of a Deal

N
W—◉—E
S

Subject
Announcement

Rajaa,

As you requested, please find below details on the I-Dimensional deal.

Summary

Type: Production

Duration: 10 years

TVC: $17.2 million

Scope: SA

Closing Date: 2/22/2007

Objective of the Mexico Closing

Objective

I-Dimensional will provide Vector with Lumina-built computers. The two required agreements with I-Dimensional—worldwide supply and IP—were negotiated in Europe and are already in place.

Sale of Assets

Assets

The purchase price for assets—production machinery, equipment, office furniture, maintenance spares and inventory—has to be settled before closing. At signing, it was estimated at $8.4M.

Goodwill
Close

Please feel free to contact me for clarification.

Regards,

Michael Morris
Mergers and Acquisitions
Vector, Inc.
michaelmorris@vector.com

Tools

Humanize technical information by dividing it up

There's no way around it—dense prose peppered with technical terms is difficult to read. One quick way to compensate for an onslaught of technicalities is by divvying the e-mail up into short paragraphs with headers. The white space relieves eyestrain and tedium, allowing the reader to skim through the document with ease.

Increase white space with indents

The more white space, the easier it is for the reader to navigate the e-mail on the screen. If you know that your e-mail program won't play havoc with indents—presenting them as indents rather than rendering them as code—you can use margins meaningfully to suggest specificity. For example, leave the broad categories flush left and indent the subjects they refer to below. Your reader will appreciate the mapping clues.

Netiquette

Money and respect tend to go together, in life as in e-mail. It makes sense, too—when millions of dollars are involved, you want the handlers to be serious, not frivolous. Large deals impact more than just bank accounts— they can directly affect millions of homes, families, and lives. Their indirect outcomes can be staggering, influencing markets, interest rates, and political opinion.

Consequently, upper-level management e-mail about deals tends to be sober and formal. In contrast to most business e-mail, where a sentence such as "Here's the data you requested" does its job admirably, in this case "as you requested, please find below," and even occasionally, "as per your request, please find below," are still holding their own.

Increased formality also extends to vocabulary, so that instead of "getting money back," you "recover costs." Similarly, the semicolon (;), whose use is generally in decline in e-mail, will often make the most of an opportunity to unite two closely related sentences in a formal e-mail, as in, "I-Dimensional has real estate and financial interests in the site; I-Dimensional makes the lease payments."

These and other markers of formal e-mail underscore the creditability, sobriety, and gravity of the communication.

Analysis of a Contract

Subject
Announcement

Agreement

Prices and
Taxes

Data
Privacy

Goodwill
Close

Doug,

I have completed my review of the Know Your Vector contract between Vector and Optimax. I list below my major concerns. I want to emphasize my concerns are really that—major.

Letter of Agreement

The Optimax T&Cs refer to a pending Letter of Agreement containing details of Optimax services, their prices, and other T&Cs. The Letter of Agreement must be reviewed to ensure there are no further Vector obligations. According to Annette, disparity exists between services as described in the Scope of Work and the services actually being performed.

Price and Taxes

The Payments Clause in the contract (and in the Scope of Work) allows Optimax some latitude to change price quotes without Vector's agreement. Because Vector usually demands more certainty in what it expects to pay, this is unacceptable.

In addition, prices exclude VAT and transport charges. Normally Vector is only liable for payments (including taxes) that are expressly stated in an invoice.

Data Privacy

Because Optimax will have access to personal information on Vector employees, we should add our standard data privacy clause.

Complimentary analysis on minor concerns will follow shortly.

Regards,

Kate Mylo
Contractions and Negotiations
Vector, Inc.
katemylo@vector.com

 *Tools*

Use present tense when referring to written documents

The present tense of "Optimax refers to a pending Letter of Agreement" is correct; the past tense of "Optimax referred to a pending letter of agreement" is not. The reasoning behind the present tense convention is a bit odd: Documents are perceived to *always* be present.

In other words, once they exist, they *always* exist—in the present. A book can be opened or a document called up on screen at any point in the future. Documents are never "past," in the sense of being finished, done with, or over. In fact, they take on—for better or worse—a kind of *eternal* aura. They are always apt to be consulted, reviewed, or reconsidered...even when the manuscripts are lost. Once a document exists, it always exists. And therefore, documents are referred to in the present tense.

Consider dropping title conventions, even in formal e-mail

Remember how you learned—or should have learned!—to put titles of chapters and short documents in double quotation marks and to italicize or underline the names of books or thick publications? For example, in hardcopy we put *The New York Times* in italics and the article "New Round of Mergers Announced" in quotes.

These rules are not always followed in business e-mail, probably because in the early days of e-mail programs, quotes and italics often ended up on the reader's screen as gobbledygook. Capitalization picks up the slack in title markers—sometimes even more capitalization than we would have in hardcopy.

Sometimes we deem "Letter of Agreement" correct. In e-mail, its now just as likely to be Letter Of Agreement. The capitals segment the reader's attention by allowing the title to stand out. And anything that stands out meaningfully in an e-mail eases the reader's comprehension.

Use Latin terms in e-mail, but use them sparingly

Interestingly enough, while many trappings of hardcopy are routinely expunged in e-mail, a few Latinisms still hang on with dignity. One is "e.g.," which means "example grata," and heads an example. Another is "i.e.," which means "in other words," and prefaces a restatement.

Less common Latinisms that might occasionally make an appearance in a business e-mail include, "viz." (namely) and "c.f." (compare and consult). Two others, "et al." (and the others) and "etc." (and so on) you probably know already.

Technical Concepts Explained

Subject
Announcement

Faris, Anne, and Souli,

In working with you lately, I've noticed that we return again and again to the topic of confidentiality. Because we are responsible for ensuring that confidentiality is appropriately handled, I thought I'd set out a few of the basics:

Confidentiality Is Consequential

Consequences

When we receive confidential information, we may face civil or criminal penalties if we fail to handle it correctly. Confidential information cannot be disclosed unless the contract warrants disclosure. Penalties include loss of confidential status (including patent rights) and/or access to our information forever. Our competitive edge is brought into risk every time we risk confidentiality. *In protecting confidentiality, Vector protects its freedom of action in developing products and services.*

Confidentiality Is An Obligation

Obligations

Signing a confidentiality agreement means taking on serious obligations. To track and communicate those obligations, the Vector recipient must implement a security plan detailing the steps Vector takes in order to comply with confidentiality. *Vector Security assists business units with these obligation plans, from development through accomplishment.*

Goodwill
Close

Confidentiality is a complex issue, and I've only touched on a few main points here. More information is contained in the list of links below. As always, I'm available to provide additional information and advice.

Regards,

Susan Timmons
Vector Legal Department
Vector, Inc.
susantimmons@vector.com

Tools

Preface each paragraph with a key-idea header

Headers can summarize, stimulate curiosity, highlight themes, and/or raise questions. Using a complete sentence containing a key idea is an elegant way of getting your message across at the same time that you map your document. Complete-sentence headers are a sure-fire way to keep both writer and reader on track.

End each short paragraph with an emphatic sentence

Prefacing a technical explanation with a header and closing it with an emphatic sentence literally adds texture to your prose. Because not all words are equal, layout style is one of the quickest strategies for segmenting the reader's attention. Use layout style to sort out which information is summary, which is substantive, and which is emphatic.

The trick is to make distinctions in emphasis function aesthetically as well. Your e-mail should please the eye, not strain it or assault it. If you use bold for the headers, use italics for the closing emphasis. If you use capitals for the headers, use underlining for the close. But be careful! A header that's bold, in capitals, underlined, and italicized is too much! Try and limit yourself to one or two stylistic effects for each emphatic unit.

Also, make sure that you use stylistic effects consistently within the same e-mail. You want your document map to be reliable! Don't use bold for summaries and then use it for the most specific, important point—that will just end up confusing the reader. The purpose of stylistic effects is to aid the reader's comprehension, not confuse it even more.

Netiquette

E-mail uses double quotation marks to draw attention to a single word. Sometimes the word is being defined, sometimes it's being called into question, and sometimes it's being used ironically. For example, in the sentence "This is our "unofficial" position," the word "unofficial" is being called into question. The reader should pause and consider what is meant by "unofficial" and why the word receives extra attention in context. In the old hardcopy days, some editors might have put the word in single quotes to draw attention to its usage, but this tendency is yielding to the double-quote solution, even, it seems, in hardcopy.

Advice on Compliance

Subject
Announcement

Consent

Negative
Change

Termination

Goodwill
Close

Alex,

On the phone yesterday, you requested advice on obtaining compliance in a compensation package remix. Here are some issues to keep in mind:

<u>Consent = written acceptance</u>. Usually we write a letter confirming the change and ask the employee to countersign for acceptance. Without consent, there is no basis for compliance.

<u>Negative changes can still receive consent</u>. Factors influencing consent include:

- the nature of the change
- the reason for the change
- mitigating circumstances

Generally speaking, if employees perceive the reasons for the change as sound, they consent, and then they can be made to comply.

<u>Vector cannot force employees to consent</u>. Employees either have to be:

- convinced by the reasons for change and consent; or
- terminated in jurisdictions where it is possible to terminate

<u>Termination requires economic, technical, or organizational justification for restructuring</u>.

If I get more precise detail about the size and nature of the change, as well as which employee groups it concerns, I will provide more precise advice.

Regards,

Lotta Bellam
Human Resource Analyst
Vector, Inc.
lottabellam@vector.com

*T*ools

Add white space to increase comprehension

The more complex the ideas are that you're communicating, the more white space your e-mail needs. White space on the screen helps structure the reader's attention to the text, allowing for pauses necessary for comprehension. The pause may be miniscule, but it counts. It is almost as if the white space says, "Let the information sink in. There! Now we're on to the next point."

Or look at it this way: If you're describing a desert landscape in detail, readers don't need lots of pauses in the writing; they will follow the ideas in the text easily because readers will see in their mind's eye the landscape as it unfolds, almost as if they were watching a movie. But there's no movie to watch when the topic is convincing employees to consent and comply with a lower salary.

White space provides reading clues, signaling to the reader that we're moving from one idea to another, or that we're looking at the topic in a different way.

Opt for simple symbols to draw attention to main points

While numbers are an appropriate structuring device, they carry hierarchical meaning that may clutter a text, send the message that some points aren't as important as others, or encourage the reader to look for sequential links that don't exist.

To mark a new point, try using a dash (—), a hyphen (-), or the business e-mail favorite—the bullet point (•). A steady climber in e-mail correspondence, the bullet point may have its command featured in a pull-down menu, even when it's also marked on the keyboard. Once confined to business reports and technical prose, the bullet point has come into its own in e-mail, precisely because it quickly communicates to the eye that a point is being made—and the reader can literally see the point, right there, heading the line. It streamlines organization because it doesn't have any residual notions of hierarchy and sequence attached to it.

When venturing further a field from the bullet point (•), stay away from shaded symbols, complicated icons, and/or cutesy thingies. The idea is to help the reader map the information in the document, not distract him or her with amateurish effects. As with a smart dresser who knows that simplicity and quality equal elegance, a well-written e-mail gets its points across without trying too hard.

Be kind to your reader

Where technical information is concerned, the readers aren't often thrilling to the depths of their emotional or spiritual being—they're trying to solve a problem. If the need to solve the problem is great enough, they'll toil through even the worse prose ever written to figure out the answer. Or they may ask you to explain it again. Or they may just give up.

But if you divvy the information into small bites, the odds are they'll get it right away. Even the most highly technical information can stimulate readers' curiosity and interest when it's presented in a way that says: You can understand this information this instant! See! It's easy!

Using white space to aid navigation, symbols to highlight changes in idea, and short sentences that process rapidly in over-taxed brains are the best ways of achieving your objective. The reader will thank you for it.

Spoon-fed readers are happy readers, because technical concepts can be hard to swallow! Literally. We've all had the experience of facing some very precise technical information—specific information that we need—and being unable to understand what we're reading. Not because we're intellectually blighted, and not because we're too lazy to concentrate long and hard enough to understand the information before us. But because technical information is, by nature, repulsive! Anytime you face something you don't understand, that requires significant effort to master, and that is alienated from your emotional being, you have to motivate yourself to get through it.

Changes in a Draft

Subject
Announcement

First
Change

Second
Change

Third
Change

Goodwill
Close

Jio,

Here are my comments on the Vector-Spark contract.

<u>P2 ¶5</u>:

I fail to see the source of the statement requiring Vector Board approval.

<u>P4 ¶7</u>:

I think Section 1.03 should be quoted somewhere, particularly the sentences, "the Parties shall file a Certificate of Merger..." and "the Merger shall become effective at such date and time...."

<u>P8 ¶1</u>:

As I said, I don't think this section helps. The relevant point is the date at which the parties are legally bound—no matter what outside conditions (including EMEA clearance) remain to be met.

It's up to you to decide if it's worth keeping.

Regards,

John Arberry
Contracts and Negotiations
Vector, Inc.
johnarberry@vector.com

$\mathcal{T}$ools

Make your changes visible when editing a draft

Writing about writing is tricky—it's like entering a house of mirrors. Sometimes it's difficult to differentiate the target text from its editing commentary. And if the commentary isn't clearly written, the process of editing can become frustrating, indeed.

Consequently, you need a fast, workable system for making changes. The primary requirement for the editing system is that it's visible. The reader should lose no time at all trying to determine if the words on the screen belong to the target text or to editing commentary.

Make a small number of changes in an e-mail, not in the draft

The reader doesn't always have to open the attachment and find the changes that you've made. It may save time to simply list the changes—provided they're not numerous—in an e-mail. That way, the reader won't omit changes in the target document if he or she scrolls through the attachment too fast.

When scrolling is involved, speed often gets the better of us. We don't see editing changes, unless care has been taken to insure that we do. It's often more efficient to simply state what changes need to be made in a separate doc.

Draw attention to the location of the changes

Explaining *where* the changes are to be made in a document is as important as explaining *what* the changes are. No editing comments are going to be worthwhile if the reader can't figure out which part of the target doc they belong to. Use white space, stylistic changes (such as boldface type), and/or color to draw attention to the location markers. Just make sure you don't overdo it, or your emphasis will get lost in busy visual effects.

Indicate the page, paragraph, and line of the changes

If you think of the target document as a kind of map, then page, paragraph, and line supply the coordinates. And just the way we abbreviate "N" for "north," we also abbreviate location markers in an editing commentary.

"P" is the best abbreviation for "page." The abbreviation is followed by the actual page numbers in the target document. No period is necessary. When more than one page is involved, "P" will still do, as in "P47-48." But in more formal e-mail documents, "pg." is still in use, as in "pg.11." The most common plural form in formal docs is "pp. 14-19."

The standard abbreviation for "paragraph" is the icon, "¶." But writing out the abbreviation "para" may be useful when you're not certain that your reader will know, or be able to ascertain, what "¶" means. Or just use P.

"L" is an acceptable abbreviation for the line location in the document when the paragraphs are long. The number of the "L" is calculated by counting down from the first line of the paragraph, not from the page.

Use an ellipsis to indicate words have been omitted

The ellipsis (…) is one of the most misunderstood marks of punctuation. It contains three dots, no more, no less. Some writers think that it means etcetera. It doesn't! The ellipse means that you're not going to waste your time recounting every word, either because it's not necessary, or because the omitted material is already clear to the reader. In the examples, "the Parties shall file a Certificate Of Merger…" and "the Merger shall become effective at such date and time…" each ellipse indicates that the sentence continues in the target text, but that it's not necessary to include every word in the commentary.

Do not lengthen your ellipsis indiscriminately

When the ellipsis coincides with the end of a sentence, it gets an extra dot (….). That means you still have three dots for the ellipsis (…) plus one (.) for the period. This is sometimes called the "3 dot-4 dot" rule.

But an ellipsis never has extra dots strung onto the end, as in ………… Long ellipses send a message of immaturity. The underage crowd who is learning to use language properly often lets the ellipsis lengthen in proportion to what the writer is unable to say. It is common to find long ellipses of variable length among grade school, high school, and undergraduate students. But as we mature as writers, we shorten our ellipses. We learn, in fact, to count our dots. If we need to indicate that the ellipsis is emphatic, we do it through the words we're using, not through cosmetic effects.

CHAPTER TEN

Run It Past Legal

INCLUDING

Legal Opinion

Legal Analysis

Legal Research

Status of Litigation

Outcome of Litigation

$\mathcal{E}$dit

Before: announcment of litigation

Taija, Dayle,

A new claim from a former supplier for Vector, who will be seeking 2.5M USD: 2M for breach of contract and 500K for unpaid bills, has just been received from the ex-supplier New City Sites. A small firm specializing in event organization New City Sites was by 2003 and perhaps before that date a Vector contractor, and in consequences of that relationship by the end of that year, it was selected and designated as a major supplier for events with a fixed-term contract that would be binding and valid until end-2006. Business was approximately 980K USD in 2004.

The documents imply and suggest that there was apparently no disagreement or conflict in evidence prior to the end of the year 2005 since Vector had even paid 650K USD up front and in advance for events on the table planned in the next year 2006, although these plans were scrapped as Vector contacted and negotiated a new event organization contract with Curators, Inc., without making any explicit commitment. Although the 2006 events planning with New City Sites was therefore quite advanced, they had however absolutely no commitment or agreement from Vector and received the de facto three-months notice as per the severance clause that was in effect making the damages claim seem completely unreasonable. Further to that fact they are still in possession of 650 K of Vector monies. I will review their bills in the near future in order to ascertain if they are valid. As this case appears straightforward, Gary Spaada of the McKenzie Law Firm would be my choice for appointment in the coming week.

Regards,

Gladys Freeport
Senior Staff Counsel
Vector, Inc.
gladysfreeport@vector.com

The problem

Attitude! Lawyers think they're good writers—after all, they've spent years and years training, reading the law and, of course, writing. They can whip out a straightforward business e-mail with no problem, right? Wrong. The training that serves them well in terms of legal expertise sometimes has a negative effect on their day-to-day communication. (But it can be difficult to convince them of that!)

Sentences! All those years of reading the law—all those long, old-fashioned sentences—contaminate many lawyers' business e-mail. They end up unconsciously imitating legal forms that are inappropriate to everyday business correspondence. Instead of sounding dynamic and vital, they risk sounding heavy and stodgy.

Wordiness! Because one word (or even one comma) can make the difference in a legal contract, lawyers try to be as precise as possible. And because they're trying to cover all the bases, they overdo, saying more than they need to just to make sure everything's covered. Heavy, ungraceful sentences result. At worst, the tendency towards wordiness clogs the sentence to the point of futility. The reader loses sight of the point the sentence is making because it's suffocated by extra words that inhibit, rather than expedite, meaning.

The solution

Transform subtle, verbal know-how into good communication habits. Because lawyers are, by nature, wordsmiths, they can easily learn to eradicate poor e-mail habits and replace them with strategies for communication that work. They have to begin by recognizing that legal prose and business e-mail use different patterns of language. We do not, for example, speak or write like statutes or contracts. Writers first have to recognize their tendency to verbosity in order to correct it.

Use an up-to-date sentence. Those long sentence patterns from the 18th-century or 19th-century, with their surfeit of commas and embedded clauses, worked well for our ancestors. Nowadays, the short sentence reigns in business e-mail. Sometimes just chopping up sentences into small units can make the difference between an e-mail that flies and one that flops.

Reign-in vocabulary. Getting rid of redundancy—and that bane of the lawyer's existence, the doublet (or triplet)—can transform clunky prose into prose that's sharp and slick. "The end of the year 2002" should be "end-2002." And "no disagreement or conflict" should be "no conflict," while "unreasonable, uncreditable, and without compelling substance" should simply be "unreasonable."

After: announcment of litigation

Taija, Dayle,

We just received a new claim from a Vector ex-supplier, New City Sites, who seeks 2.5M USD: 2M for breach of contract and 500K for unpaid bills.

Background

New City Sites is a small firm specializing in event organization. By 2004—and perhaps before—it was a Vector contractor. By end-2004, it was selected as a major supplier for events, apparently with a fixed-term contract until end-2006. Their business was 980K USD in 2004.

As far as I can see, there was no conflict prior to end-2005. Vector had even paid 650K USD in advance for events planned in 2006. But due to a decision made by upper level management, Vector negotiated a new event-organization contract with Curators, Inc., without making any commitment to New City Sites. In addition, there was no attempt to recuperate the 650K.

Risk Assessment

Although the 2006 events planning with New City Sites was quite advanced, they had no commitment from Vector. They received the de facto three-months notice. Thus the damages claim seems completely unreasonable.

But they are still in possession of 650K of Vector monies. I am in the process of reviewing their bills.

Selection of Outside Counsel

Because this case appears straightforward, my recommendation is to appoint Gary Spaada of the McKenzie Law Firm in the coming week.

Gladys Freeport
Senior Staff Counsel
Vector, Inc.
gladysfreeport@vector.com

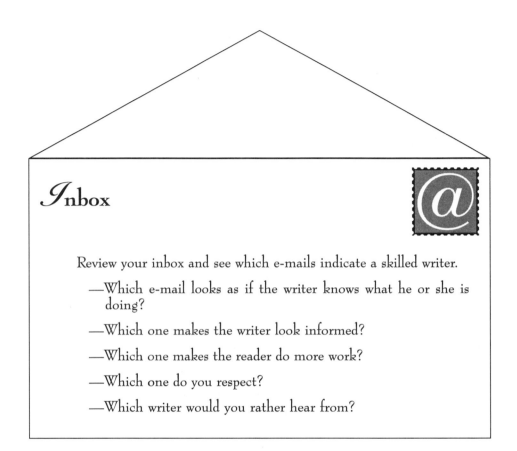

*I*nbox

Review your inbox and see which e-mails indicate a skilled writer.

—Which e-mail looks as if the writer knows what he or she is doing?

—Which one makes the writer look informed?

—Which one makes the reader do more work?

—Which one do you respect?

—Which writer would you rather hear from?

Legal Opinion

Subject
Announcement

Goodwill Close

Jody, Ebbe, Syd,

To explain differences between Nordic and Anglo-American legal drafting, I offer the following legal opinion on settlements and releases. Please see the attached document for a detailed analysis.

Please let me know if I can clarify further.

Francois Lopez
Senior Litigation Counsel
Vector Dimensional
francoislopez@vector.com

Sample text from attached document

Standard template and release letters do not exist in the Nordics. The scope, form and content of material settlement are subject to detailed negotiations in which principles of Nordic Law significantly vary from the Anglo-American.

The Anglo-American tradition favors legal specification while Nordic legal tradition favors broad legal standards. For example, in the Anglo-American tradition parties would be defined as:

> *Themselves, their predecessors, executors, administrators, heirs, successors, assigns, agents, attorneys, insurers, representatives, and all parent, subsidiary, predecessor, successor, and related corporations, and all officers, directors, shareholders, members, partners, and employees, and all persons acting through, under, or in concert with them or any of them.*

In the Nordics, we simply use "the parties," since interpretation of the term "parties" is established by the legal rules governing a settlement.

Tools

Divide long legal e-mails into a personalized preface and an impersonal document

The firm's legal department straddles two worlds: one business, one legal. Often e-mails to other lawyers or to clients in the firm are complex, lengthy, and specialized. The convention of announcing a subject, giving information on the subject, then issuing a goodwill close doesn't work well with long, technical documents. It looks as if the document has been sandwiched arbitrarily in the e-mail between a hello and goodbye.

Consequently, it's better to preface a technical document in a short, annunciatory note and then follow the note with the specialized text, either pasted-in or attached. That way, the writer and the information remain visually separate, a division which is appropriate in a field based on separating analysis and reasoning from emotion and feeling.

Mirror the organization of short e-mails in long documents

A short e-mail announces its subject, makes a few points about it, then closes. The same thing holds true of longer e-mails.

The longer text has one subject dominating the information hierarchy. The main points about the subject provide the structure of the text. Sometimes each of these main points leads off a separate section, composed, in turn, of supporting points. The sections sometimes turn their points into headers.

What this amounts to is the following: The subject of the text stands out; the main points stand out; and in some cases the main points are themselves composed of supporting points. Identifying, emphasizing, and structuring information according to hierarchical importance ensures a mapped document that keeps the writer on track. It allows readers to locate the specific information they need.

Use a combination of underlining, bold, italics, and capitals to segment the reader's attention

If the information is coming by e-mail, then it's got to have a strong layout, no matter how long (or short!) the document is.

A printed document doesn't have to cater to readers in the same way for many reasons, including the fact that readers turn pages, they don't scroll. The text is continually broken up in a book—by a turned page, or by the eye wandering from the edge of the page to the window. Not so in e-mail. The eye is framed by the screen and the window; the more the reader scrolls, the greater the risk of inattention.

To make the readers' job—and yours—easier, subtitle your sections, italicize and indent long quotes, and pull out the bullet points for the list at the end. Segment the reader's attention with layout cues. (Or risk having your text blur into one long blah-blah-blah!) But do *something* to map the document, or the chances are the recipients won't read with much comprehension or interest. He or she may not even read it all.

Options

I offer this opinion...

I forward you this opinion...

I am happy to supply you with this opinion...

I am pleased to contribute a legal opinion...

I have written a legal opinion on the subject...

I am furnishing you with my legal opinion...

I am providing you with my legal opinion...

CEOs usually write quite well

Some of the best writers I've come across sit on the boards of international firms. We don't often see their work on the shelves in bookstores, but they could write successful books if they wanted to.

Legal Analysis

Subject
Announcement

Goodwill
Close

Carl, Racey,

Please find below our analysis of the Optimax case.

We look forward to discussing the information in detail.

Violette Osaleen
Senior Counsel, Competition Law
violetteosaleen@vector.com

Sample text from attached document

ASSESSMENT SUMMARY
OF OPTIMAX'S CLAIMS

Optimax's recent advertising claims against Vector Poetics in their WebNet ads and on their Website are contradicted by Software Imaging Study data, third-party data and the Software Customer Satisfaction Diagnostic data. *Most data oppose Optimax's claims.*

Software Imaging Study data on the consideration, preference, and penetration of Web Application Server Software and e-Business Software platforms favors Vector. The study findings are consistent with third party sources (i.e., Marks Mind). Our internal Customer Satisfaction data neither contradicts nor supports Optimax's claims, where Optimax's WebNet outperforms Vector's Poetics on four attributes:

- Overall Satisfaction
- Performance
- Reliability
- Installability

Ultimately the margins are much lower than Optimax's ad suggests, and we tie on with the majority of attributes.

Tools

Divide your document into main ideas and supporting points

Not all documents have the same structure. Some documents are built from complicated hierarchies of information, while others are more straightforward and traditional—the difference, say, between a cathedral and cabin. In some documents, main points and supporting points alternate in a magisterial give-and-take of stunning complexity, while in others, the main ideas and supporting points align themselves in a pleasing, accessible symmetry.

To determine the structure of your document, identify main ideas and supporting points. Then fill out the structure with insights, details, examples, and commentary. Filling out is the easy part.

The hard part is reducing your ideas to an armature in which the hierarchy of information is clear. The ability to identify main ideas and supporting points separates the maestros from the wannabes.

Group information to determine the main ideas

If you're having trouble separating main ideas from supporting points, key-in everything you can think of about your topic in one-liners. Then sort the lines into groups based on similarity. Your main ideas are the glue that holds the groups together.

Modulate the reader's attention by changing typographic styles from bold to Roman

Using boldface for main-idea paragraphs and Roman type for paragraphs with supporting points aids and abets skimming. Some higher-ups just want the main ideas; those who are more hands-on will want to comb through the supporting points, too. Changing typographic styles helps them find the information they want and skip the information that they don't need.

Reserve italics for secondary emphasis—the supporting points that shouldn't be missed

Italics have a kind of understated impact in a formal document. They don't shout, like capitals. They don't insist, like bold face. They're like a lowered voice at the punch line: *Everyone leans in to hear.*

Reinforce reading cues with indents

Anchor the most important, or most general, text on the left-hand margin—the main ideas. Indent the supporting points in boldface type by 5–7 spaces. Less significant, but necessary, details are indented again.

The deeper the indent, the more detailed the information.

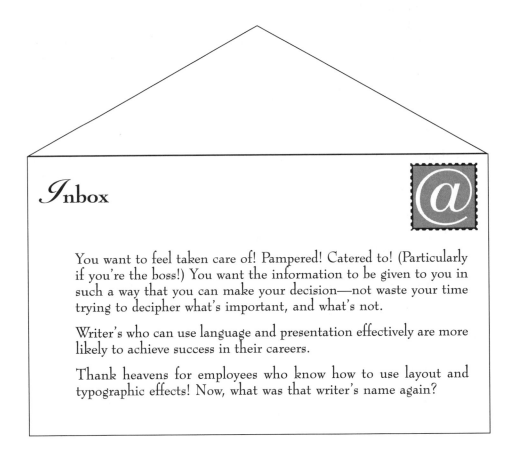

*𝒥*nbox

You want to feel taken care of! Pampered! Catered to! (Particularly if you're the boss!) You want the information to be given to you in such a way that you can make your decision—not waste your time trying to decipher what's important, and what's not.

Writer's who can use language and presentation effectively are more likely to achieve success in their careers.

Thank heavens for employees who know how to use layout and typographic effects! Now, what was that writer's name again?

Legal Research

Subject
Announcement

Goodwill
Close

Conrad,

Here's the redux of the NAD.

Let me know if you need more.

Sherif Cinnel
Vector Legal Department
sherifcinnel@vector.com

Sample text from attached document

NATIONAL ADVERTISING DIVISION (NAD) OF THE BETTER BUSINESS BUREAU

Definition

The National Advertising Division of the Better Business Bureau (NAD) and the National Advertising Review Board (NARB) are set up as the advertising industry's self-regulatory bodies.

Proceedings

NAD can institute proceedings based on a complaint from a competitor, consumer or consumer group, and they can also initiate their own investigation. The entire process (with an appeal) normally takes 3 to 4 months.

Our Option

Because NAD focuses on market research, the TD attorney strongly advocates engaging an independent market research firm with credibility at NAD to conduct a study on customer perceptions of the Optimax ad.

Tools

Use "definition" to explain what a thing is and how it works

The rhetorical mode of "definition" is suited to describing, classifying, and explaining. The trick in definition is the arrangement of information, from the most general to the most specific. Sometimes referred to as the "funnel" method, definition begins broadly, and then narrows towards the end.

Consider using definition to structure an entire text, a paragraph, and/or a sentence

As with other writing patterns—such as, comparison and contrast, explanation, narration, and description—definition can be adapted to any level of organization within a text. You can define a term broadly in the first paragraph, less broadly in the second, and so on, until you arrive at the fifth paragraph focusing on a specific example.

Or you can apply the same principle to paragraph construction. The first sentence classifies the term broadly, the second sentence narrows the definition, and so on. At the level of the sentence, definition dispenses information quickly so that the reader can understand how a particular term is being used in the surrounding text.

Blend definition with other writing patterns

E-mails frequently combine writing patterns to get their job done. An e-mail may begin with definition, say, and after spending several paragraphs defining the term with greater and greater precision, end up with a paragraph of narrative cause-and-effect.

Combining different writing patterns, such as analysis and description, or narrative chronology and explanation, is the mark of a confident writer. Short e-mail can often get by using one pattern, such as chronological narration, while longer texts often require patterns in combination.

Notice which pattern you're using

Writing skill depends, to a large degree, on conscious control. Writers who are comparing and contrasting options for legal retaliation put the similarities between options in one paragraph and the differences in another. In the same way, a writer narrating recent developments in a sales campaign may follow a paragraph of chronology with a paragraph of description.

Being aware of *how* you're writing, instead of just *what* you're writing, makes an important difference in the quality of your copy. Strong writers never lose sight of the *how*, while weak writers tend to focus too much on the *what*. The content of your prose never gets to shine unless you make it visible. Your ideas may be brilliant, but if you can't communicate them, they'll never be recognized or acknowledged.

$\mathcal{N}$etiquette

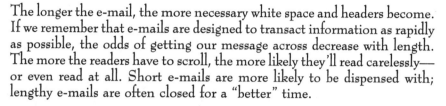

The longer the e-mail, the more necessary white space and headers become. If we remember that e-mails are designed to transact information as rapidly as possible, the odds of getting our message across decrease with length. The more the readers have to scroll, the more likely they'll read carelessly— or even read at all. Short e-mails are more likely to be dispensed with; lengthy e-mails are often closed for a "better" time.

All the more reason to encourage readers with generous white space and headers. They can scan, zoom to the best part, and skip at will. And if the headers are doing their job, the reader can just skim the headers and still have a pretty clear idea of the information that the document contains. Instead of being weighty and foreboding, a long e-mail structured with white space and headers seems less burdensome, even welcoming. The white space and headers assure readers that their comprehension is paramount, and that their precious time won't be wasted.

Just as importantly, document structure plays an important role in memory. Because memory works by emphasis—things that standout are more likely to be remembered than things that blend in—a well-structured document has more chance of making memorable points than one in which all the information seems equal. Readers will probably remember the indented point in **BOLDFACE CAPITALS**; the point made in the third sentence of the fifth paragraph, they probably won't.

Status of Litigation

N
W — E
S

Subject Announcement

Narrative 1

Narrative 2

Observations

Goodwill Close

Ed, Lucia,

I have much to report regarding the recent Lumina litigation that may affect us.

As you may have heard, the judge in the case recently ordered a settlement discussion among Jayne, Anselm, and Bob. It was to precede discussions between the Vector and Lumina teams, scheduled for the first week in June. But the settlement discussion failed. Simply put: Lumina's current demands are completely out of line.

Last week, on June 16, the Court heard Lumina's motion for preliminary injunction in which Lumina asked the Court to remove our Metric Locator System software from the marketplace. The hearing went as expected. While we never know what the court will do, it is clear that the Judge had read our materials, seemed to understand the issues and asked sharp questions that obviously put Lumina on the defensive.

The team has worked very hard to do everything humanly possible to win this motion. I remain cautiously optimistic about our chance for success. The Judge hasn't told us when he plans to rule, but it probably won't be before July.

If you have any questions, please give me a call.

Jenny Dern
Corporate Law Attorney
Vector, Inc.
jennydern@vector.inc

Tools

Alternate sentence patterns to give your prose texture

Most writers tend to favor one kind of sentence style over another. The preferred sentence style may be clear and concise, but when it's used over and over, it can lead to a monotonous rhythm in the paragraph and in the document. A monotonous rhythm, in turn, compromises readers' attentiveness, lulling them into boredom instead of sparking their interest. This is the reason why writers should pay attention to their sentence patterns: to keep their readers active.

Don't confuse variable sentence patterns with muddled prose

The first rule of thumb is clarity and concision. You need to get your ideas across efficiently in as few a words as possible. Once competency is reached in short sentences, the next step is to combine them in longer units. (But never heavy, convoluted ones!) Lastly, serious writers reach the stage when they can alternate short and long sentence patterns to achieve an interesting rhythm and texture in their prose.

Try following a long sentence unit with a short, tight one

Different sentence patterns elicit different reading strategies. In a long sentence, the reader eases from the introductory clause into the main clause, and progresses through extended complements. While in a short sentence, the reader can take in the whole thing at a glance.

In the following example, a long sentence is followed by a short, brisk one: "Last week, on June 16, the Court heard Lumina's motion for preliminary injunction in which Lumina asked the Court to remove our Metric Locator System software from the marketplace. The hearing went as expected." The first sentence unit required more sustained concentration than the second; together they deliver a kind of one-two punch, in which the short sentence benefits from the release of the previous sentence unit. It gets the bounce.

Try stringing together a couple or even a few long sentences and follow them by a short, crisp one. Your shorter sentence will get a little extra emphasis and your reader will appreciate the change of pace.

Mix sentence styles to give your prose texture

The following paragraph combines four different sentence patterns:

> *As you may have heard, the judge in the case recently ordered a settlement discussion among Jay, Ray, and Julio (introductory clause, main clause). It was to precede discussions between the Vector and Lumina teams, scheduled for the first week in June (main clause, subordinate clause). But the settlement discussion failed (main clause prefaced by a conjunction). Simply put: Lumina's current demands are completely out of line (Main clause prefaced by introductory phrase and colon).*

The variations in sentence pattern segment the reader's attention and generate interest, while the same old sentence patterns are exactly that— the same old sentence patterns. Variation in sentence patterns keeps readers sharp; monotonous sentence patterns allow their attention to flag.

Don't forget to vary punctuation, too

The conscientious use of a dash, a colon, or even a semicolon gives your sentences instant pizzazz. And question marks and quotation marks can also spruce up the monotony of the same old comma and period. Punctuation adds texture, verve, and subtly to your ideas—provided you use it correctly and don't overdo it!

Options

As we discussed...

You've no doubt heard the news that...

As you may have heard...

You're probably aware that...

As you probably know...

I'm sure you know...

As I mentioned before...

As you'll probably remember...

Outcome of Litigation

Jack,

Subject
Announcement

Today we received the Appellate level judgment in the 4-year-old Height Corp. case against Optimax and Vector.

Prior
Litigation

The case relates to Optimax's 2003 decision to defer Ode 2.5 development and delivery schedule. No damages were awarded against Optimax.

Current
Litigation

In its decision, the Appellate Court reversed the counterclaim. It awarded Height Corp. 3.6M USD in damages; ordered Optimax to repay Height Corp. 0.6M for Vector services rendered; and reimburse 0.1M USD of Height Corp's legal fees.

Damages

The 3.6M USD in damages obtained today by Height Corp. represents roughly 1% of its total damage claim of 378M USD, virtually all of it comprised of indirect damages, such as lost profits and lost savings.

But in an absolutely critical part of its decision, the court upheld Optimax's limitation of liability provisions. It capped Height Corp.'s claimed damages of 378M USD at the maximum of 3.6 M USD for the more than 7-month delay.

Liability

Vector was not found liable in any manner, and thus has no obligation to pay damages.

Both parties have two months to file an appeal. I will make a recommendation once I have read a full translation of the decision, but my instinct is that this is too good an outcome to risk in an appeal. It is unclear to me how HC will reason in this matter.

Cody Visse
Senior Litigation Counsel
Vector, Inc
codyvisse@vector.com

Tools

Try not to write in legalese

Legalese is the term for a kind of English heavily influenced by the style and vocabulary of legal documents. Because legal documents are historical artifacts, the language is historical, too. Lawyers spend so much time reading that they risk assimilating—and using—old-fashioned language patterns in inappropriate contexts. The resulting e-mail is usually heavy, cumbersome, and stodgy.

Recognize the difference between a formal e-mail style and a turgid one

E-mail can be written in a high formal style that is authoritative and decisive without being pretentious and stuffy. The key is using up-to-date, objective language—the kind of language that we come across in crisp, authoritative English-language newspapers and Websites. Rational, not emotional. Clear, not muddled. Sober, not self-important. Long, complex sentences and lofty vocabulary are tip-offs that the writing is veering in the wrong direction.

Remember that lawyers complain about other lawyers' writing

Sometimes lawyers make the mistake of thinking: I write for lawyers—so only those outside of the legal profession have trouble understanding me. *Nothing could be further from the truth*. Lawyers who are clear communicators are the first to criticize their long-winded peers. Pull them aside, and they may even *cringe* while divulging their honest thoughts about their colleagues' prose.

Lawyers who write well realize that there's a difference between jargon (the technical vocabulary of a specific field) and verbosity (turgid language). Expert communicators may have to use words and concepts specific to the legal field, but they do so in such a way that clarity maintains the upper hand. Instead of writing that "Said 'nolo contendere' plea was entered by said claimant in the aforementioned cause of action," a good communicator writers, "The claimant pleaded 'no contest' in the lawsuit."

Lawyers who are poor communicators typically blame the readers instead of themselves.

CHAPTER ELEVEN

On a Personal Note

INCLUDING

Consoling Coworkers

Expressing Sympathy

Get Well Soon

Personal Congratulations

Personal Thanks

$\mathcal{A}$dvice

E-mails that feel, e-mails that don't

We've all received an e-mail that made us smile, or that made us feel disappointed, or even angry. Although the feelings generated by e-mail are real, they are difficult to pinpoint, much less analyze. Many readers, for example, would say that "I'm sorry" is more emotional than "I regret." But not all readers would agree that "update" is less neutral than "information." Or that when introducing components in a list, a bullet point (•) is more objective and less humanistic than a dash (—).

The emotional tenor of an e-mail depends on:

—the relationship between writer and reader, including how long they've known one another, how congenial the relationship is, and the social and professional hierarchies imposed on the e-mail transaction

—the context in which the e-mail is written, including time constraints and the position of the e-mail in the sequence of the e-mail thread

—the subject matter

—the layout, organization, sentence patterns, punctuation, and word choice

—the conscientiousness, sensitivity, and mood of the writer

—the conscientiousness, sensitivity, and mood of the reader

All these factors—and others—equilibrate and synchronize as the e-mail is read. The writer can control some things, such as which features of the subject matter to emphasize and which aspects of the subject matter to downplay. But the reader's mood upon opening the e-mail—stressed, exhausted, relaxed, jovial—is not within the writer's purview. And the social and professional hierarchy inherent in the relationship is something the writer cannot change.

How can writers control the emotions generated by their e-mails? The answer is that they can't. They can only be conscious of, and pay attention to, the factors they *can* control—timing, layout, sentence patterns, word choice, and so on. For example, writers should recognize that an all-caps run-on sentence with SMS acronyms generates different emotional values than one written with normative capitalization and professional vocabulary. In the same way, an e-mail that begins "I feel that…" strikes a different tone than "I think that…."

Although most of the time, business e-mail favors an emotionally neutral there are cases when emotional generosity is highly desirable. When a coworker has suffered a loss or a hardship, when a coworker has received a distinction or a reward, or when a coworker deserves thanks for extra support, then even the sharpest business personality should reveal a softer, gentler side.

The emotive quality of personal e-mail emerges from:

—usage of the "I" pronoun

—markers of familiarity, such as first names and shared memories

Consider, for example, the difference between, "It is very unfortunate to hear of your husband's unexpected death" with "I was saddened by the news of Robert's passing." In the second sentence, the "I" pronoun combined with the emotional word "saddened"; the name of the deceased, "Robert"; and choice of the euphemistic "passing" instead of the bald word "death" generate sincerity and compassion in the emotional tone.

But it is sometimes difficult for business writers to switch from their habitual, business-like writing style to a more personalized one. The crisp and confident professional persona might be reluctant to admit messier, less predictable, emotions. All the more reason to consciously make the effort to communicate how you feel.

Personal e-mail in a business context is never gushy, or even overtly affectionate, but it is friendly, kind, and compassionate. Your reader will be touched that you were willing to reveal the part of you that feels deeply…even if it only lasts a sentence or two!

Do…

Send your social e-mail promptly.

Mention the specific reason you're writing—loss, hardship, award, or simply saying thank you.

Adopt a personable, informal tone.

Imagine what you'd want to hear if you changed places with the reader.

Don't…

Put off sending social e-mail because it's difficult to write.

Avoid referring to yourself in the first person.

Omit reference to the situation that occasioned the e-mail.

Hide behind a business-as-usual persona.

Consoling Coworkers

Natural Disaster

Sya,

Expression of Sympathy

Specific Offer

Follow Up

I am very sorry to hear about the damage to your property in the recent fires. It must be a very difficult time for you and your family. I would be happy to loan you a car if it's helpful. Or if you need a hand salvaging, please let me know. I'll check back soon to see how things are going.

Cor Pirensi
Sales Development Director
Vector, Inc.
corpirensi@vector.com

Natural Disaster

Pablo,

Expression of Sympathy

Commisaration

Encouragement

I was sad to learn your family has been hit by the recent floods. It is a horrible thing to go through, as I learned a few years ago when I lived in the flood path of the Mississippi. I remember feeling utterly powerless, and then finding, somehow, the courage to rebuild. You'll get through this. Please phone me if you'd like to talk.

Henri Attia
Associate MIS Director
Vector, Inc.
henriattia@vector.com

Victim of Crime

Columbe,

Expression of Sympathy

I just found out from Sid that your house was robbed and ransacked while we were at the IT conference. I'm at a loss as to what to say, other than to express my heartfelt sympathy.

Specific Offer

I would be happy to contact the insurance companies and security company on your behalf—you could say that I have experience in this area! And please feel free to use my name

Follow Up

if it'll help. I'll give you a call to see if there's anything I can do to help.

Peter Mahoun
Director of Corp. Underwriting
Vector, Inc.
petermahoun@vector.com

*T*ools

Refer to the hardship quickly without going into detail

You don't want to mention that the Mercedes was overturned and slammed into a pylon or that there's a dune of ashes where the den used to be. The idea is to acknowledge the hardship, not dwell on it.

Console the reader, if possible, by referring to your own experience with hardship

If you've had a similar experience, mention it to the reader and offer to discuss the details. The reader will take consolation in the fact that you've weathered a comparable tragedy and lived to tell the tale.

Make a concrete offer of assistance

Choose something realistic that you really can do—don't offer to house a family of four if you can't. Sometimes little things, such as making a phone call or lending a contact, can make a huge difference to someone recovering from hardship.

*O*ptions

I was sad to learn...

I am very sorry to hear about...

I was unhappy to learn...

I was very worried when I heard that...

I was shocked to hear...

I was distressed to learn...

I would like to offer my sympathy for your recent hardship...

Please accept my sympathy for your recent hardship...

Sloppy writing is egoistic

If you don't make an effort to write clearly, you are unconsciously telling the reader that you can't be bothered. (The reader has to figure out what you couldn't figure out yourself.)

If you don't take the time to efficiently structure an e-mail, you're signaling that your time is more precious than the reader's. (The reader has to take time on the other end to prioritize the information.)

If you're not fastidious enough to clean up minor mistakes before sending, then you're telling the reader that you don't care how you look on paper. (The reader has to take time to consciously decipher the errors.)

Ineffective writing strategies negate the fact that communication is a two-way channel. Relinquishing your responsibility as a writer puts the burden of comprehension on the reader. This makes you look bad.

Expressing Sympathy

To Coworker

*Expression of
Sympathy*

Specific Offer

Alyce,

I am deeply sorry to hear of your loss. Donal's passing must have been a shock. Give yourself time to recover. If I can take over any of your workload, please know that I am ready to do so. You are in my thoughts.

Mica Lair
Creative Services Coordinator
Vector, Inc.
micalair@vector.com

To Partner/Family of Deceased Coworker

*Expression of
Sympathy
Direct
Reference*

*Formal
Condolences*

Jenn,

I want you to know how badly I feel at this difficult time. Everet's loss saddens us all. He was a close colleague, one who I will miss daily. I will always remember his consideration toward his coworkers and his elevator jokes, which make me smile even now. Please accept my deepest condolences.

Dowa Anaganostopolus
Financial Analyst
Vector, Inc.
dowaaganostopolus@vector.com

$\mathcal{A}$dvice

Don't wait to send your sympathy e-mail

Within 24-hours of learning of a death, you should mail a brief sympathy e-mail. If you wait longer than that, you should write, well, a *longer* e-mail. A brief e-mail that arrives a month after the fact looks as if you put off writing the note, perhaps out of your own inability to deal with the tragedy. But if you did find out the news well after the services have taken place, then you should explain so in your e-mail. That way, it doesn't look like emotional immaturity held you back.

Don't mention the details of the death

Refer to "loss" or "passing," but skip the particulars, even when the death is a result of a long illness.

Focus your e-mail on your personal connection

If you were close to the person who died, then your e-mail to the partner/ family should draw attention to the relationship you had with the deceased. If you didn't really know the deceased, but know the bereaved, then your e-mail should focus on him or her.

Include a pleasant detail about the deceased

In many ways, death is about memory. Those who knew the deceased archive memories of him or her and play them back, so to speak, during bereavement. Some little detail, a characteristic the deceased had, an incident or event that struck you as telling, is literally the heart of your sympathy e-mail.

If you knew the deceased well, this is the place where your e-mail can expand. Recount a memory you have of sharing time with the deceased; if you were very close, and spent a lot of time together, then recount two or three telling memories. It will help you personally process the death as well as comfort the bereaved with the knowledge that the deceased touched the lives of others.

Acknowledge grief

Including a thoughtful sentence acknowledging the family's shock, difficulty, sadness, or pain sends a message of compassion, while the inability to verbalize awareness of another's grief suggests immaturity. But side-stepping grief—yours or someone else's—out of embarrassment doesn't relieve anyone of suffering. Sharing grief, on the other hand, helps to lessen its burden.

Offer to do something specific for the bereaved

The idea here is to choose something concrete—water someone's plants while they're out of the office, offer to ferry things to and from the house, take over part of someone's workload. And do it.

Send flowers or contribute to the memorial fund

But don't expect this gesture to substitute for your empathy note! Out of respect to the deceased, you still have to write it to the bereaved.

Don't expect your sympathy note, flowers, or contribution to be acknowledged

Amid the emotional shock and institutional demands of death, the bereaved won't have time or energy to acknowledge few, if any, of the notes they've received. But like the turnstile at the doorway, they will remember who sent a sympathy note. Even bereaved in the throes of emotional shock have an uncanny ability to tally those friends and acquaintances who verbalized their compassion. And those who didn't.

Follow-up eventually with a short how-are-coping e-mail or phone call

The aftermath of death has its own rhythm in the lives of the bereaved. Mourning may well intensify long after the memorial services have concluded. A very brief e-mail or phone call reminding the bereaved that you're thinking of them can make a huge difference in their lives, even when—or especially when—you're not particularly close to the family. It's proof, once again, that the deceased had friends and acquaintances who remember.

The importance of structure

Structure helps the *reader* quickly find the information that he or she wants from a document. Structure helps the *writer* quickly organize the document.

Get Well Soon

Surgery

Sal,

Expression of Sympathy

I just found out that you've had to undergo surgery. I imagine it isn't much fun! Do what the doctors say, and you'll recover soon. We're holding down the office until you get back. Let me know how you are when you get a chance.

Goodwill Close

Victor Naples
Market Concept Analyst
Vector, Inc.
victornaples@vector.com

Accident

Jay-Lin,

Encouragement

I was surprised to learn that you've broken your leg during your skiing trip. Hap told me though that the outlook is quite favorable, and that you should make a full recovery in the coming weeks. If you're as good at mending bone as you are at crunching numbers, I'm sure you'll be back in the office in no time. Until then, let me know if I help with the telecommute.

Cheerful Observation

Goodwill Close

Fran Suki
Financial Officer
Vector, Inc.
fransuki@vector.com

Illness

Homer,

Goodwill Statement

I am so sorry to hear of your recent illness. If there's anything I can do to help at work or at home, please don't hesitate to let me know. Be thankful that you've at least been given a reprieve from the budget meeting on Friday! I wish you a rapid recovery.

Cheerful Observation

Nan Ventoux
Deputy Director, Information Manager Systems
Vector, Inc.
nanventoux@vector.com

*A*dvice

Send your get-well-soon e-mail right away

Sometimes people get better faster than we anticipate. Be prepared to turn your get-well into a congratulations-on-your-quick-recovery if you lag too far behind!

Don't confuse sympathy with pity

The line between sympathy and pity can be thinly drawn. Sympathy makes us feel better—Edet cares, Antonio took the time to e-mail me, Matt noticed I wasn't at work.

Pity has the opposite effect: it makes us feel embarrassed and perhaps sorry for ourselves. Pity occurs when we overdo sympathy—not simply acknowledging someone's illness, but dwelling on the circumstances, pain, suffering.

While death and hardship are often out of our hands, there is often a residual sense that people are somehow to blame for their own illnesses, almost as if they willed them to happen. This way of thinking may be hogwash, but the guilt that attaches to being ill isn't.

Overachievers in particular often have a tough time being ill. The weakness and vulnerability associated with an ill body contradict the go-and-get-'em persona projected at work. For that reason, briefly mention the illness, but avoid the particulars. The last thing an ill overachiever needs to worry about is office gossip regarding the gory details.

Include a cheerful observation whenever possible

A too-bad-you-missed-the-budget-meeting line lightens up a get-well e-mail and shifts the focus away from misfortune. A playful, light-hearted observation is often one of the best reminders that this, too, shall pass.

Offer to do something, even if you don't know the reader well

The best policy is to offer to do something concrete—pick-up organic juice from a particular grocer, schlep over work from the office, or make an important phone call. But if you feel awkward making a specific offer, then opt for the banal, "if you need anything, let me know" option. Your offer probably won't be taken up, but your goodwill will be appreciated.

For the reader, not the writer

—The reader should be readily able to understand an e-mail.

—The reader should be able to instantly locate the main point of the e-mail.

—The reader should not have to decode or decipher an e-mail.

—The reader should not ask for clarification because of poor writing skills.

—The reader should not be burdened with repetitious ideas or sentences.

—The reader should not confront basic grammar or spelling mistakes.

—The reader should feel welcomed by a document.

—The reader should feel as if he or she has learned something after reading the e-mail.

Personal Congratulations

Marriage

Mia,

Achievement

Enthusiasm

I'm writing to tell you how happy I am to hear your good news! Congratulations on your recent marriage. I'm certain it's going to be a wonderful, new phase of life for you. I wish you all the best.

Chao Thorn
Business Unit Manager
Vector, Inc.
chaothorn@vector.com

Award

Jess,

Achievement

Congratulations on your Better Business For The New Economy nomination! This is a fitting tribute to your accomplishments here at Vector and in the community. I am very happy that your achievements have been acknowledged

Outcome

by your business peers. I am forwarding the announcement of your nomination to Vector Direct so readers on the intranet

Goodwill

Close

can applaud your accomplishment, too.

Colin Corel
Director, Operations and Strategy
Vector, Inc.
colincorel@vector.inc

$\mathcal{T}$ools

Allow yourself an exclamation point...or even two!

Congratulations e-mails are as likely an opportunity as ever for exclamation points. As markers of enthusiasm, intensity, and surprise, the exclamation point is far more personal than other marks of punctuation. No semicolon will ever be as heartfelt or as genuine.

An exclamation point at the beginning of the e-mail sets a buoyant tone and resonates throughout the text, while an exclamation at the end has all the fanfare of a positive send-off. Exclamation points can also close compliments and good wishes, or declarations of heightened emotion. They're like a friendly pat on the back! They feel good!!

But, as always, don't overdo it. Too many exclamation marks conflict with one another. Rather than augmenting heartfelt intensity, they can have the opposite effect—calling easy, excessive emotion in question.

Keep your congratulations e-mail to the point

As with other personal business e-mail, three or four sentences are all you need. State what the accomplishment is so that it's clear to the reader that you know what you're talking about. Then modify the accomplishment in one or two sentences—express your enthusiasm, amplify the significance, and/or draw attention to the pay off of hard work. Conclude the e-mail by expressing your goodwill and/or good wishes.

Don't horn in on someone else's congratulations e-mail

While it's a standard writing strategy to refer to your own trials and tribulations when acknowledging a coworker's hardship, it's in poor taste when it comes to a congratulations e-mail. Sharing a burden lessens it, but hogging the limelight makes you look jealous, insecure, or egotistical— or perhaps all three. Focus on the reader in a congratulations e-mail, not on yourself.

Relay the good news to others

Sometimes your coworkers will be loath to toot their own horn, even when it's to their advantage. Showing off is one thing, acknowledging the results of hard work or even good luck is another. If the good news should be passed around the company, do it. Department newsletters, intranet publications, and meeting announcements are potential sources of diffusion. Your coworker will probably be relieved that someone else took the initiative while you will benefit from building camaraderie in the firm.

Personal Thanks

Christmas Gift

Heraton,

I want to thank you for the wonderful Christmas gift you left in my office. The Calendar of Ancient Monuments and Antiquities is perfect! Please know that your kind thoughtfulness is appreciated.

Catherine Heally
Compensation Analyst
Vector, Inc.
catherineheally@vector.com

Express Thanks

Appreciation
Gratitude

Impromptu Gift

Sergio,

This is just to thank you for the playoff tickets. I wasn't aware that you knew of my fanaticism in this area! I'll give you a full report after the game. Thanks again.

Anya Ralavitch
IT Systems Coordinator
Vector, Inc.
anyaralavitch@vector.com

Appreciation

Gratitude

Coming to the Rescue

Camille,

Express Thanks

Appreciation
Promise

I want to thank you for loaning me your backup computer yesterday. I was in a real jam in terms of the Strategic Initiatives deadline, and you saved the day. Please count on me to do you a good turn when you need it.

August Rollins
Business Strategy Consultant
Vector, Inc.
augustrollins@vector.inc

Coming to the Rescue

Bill,

Situation

Gratitude

Appreciation

Thanks for covering for me at work yesterday. I was so ill from the bad food at the buffet that there was no way I could even sit at my desk. The timing could not have been worse. Please know that I really appreciated your help!

Dorothy Worden
Sales Management Director
Vector, Inc.
dorothyworden@vector.com

Tools

Keep your thank-you note brief

Thank-you notes follow simple formulae. Thank-you notes for gifts name the gift in the first sentence; describe appreciation for the gift in the second and third sentences; and reiterate gratitude in the close.

Thank-you notes for services that coworkers rendered have a similar pattern: explicit reference to the service in the first sentence; either a description of the situation or explicit appreciation in the second and third sentence; and reiteration of gratitude in the close.

Don't thank someone for something in just two sentences

Referring to the gift or service in the first sentence, and expressing gratitude in the second isn't enough! You need to say something about the gift or service, even if it's the proverbial necktie that you'll never wear. Find some aspect of the gift that's praiseworthy, or explain why the service was necessary. If you don't take the time to describe a feature or characteristic of a gift—or mention, say, the timeliness of the service—you risk looking more dutiful than gracious.

Remember that social skills are the key to success

A thank-you e-mail takes a few minutes, but the impression it makes can last for years. You want to be known as civilized and cultured, not clueless and self-centered. If someone goes out of his or her way for you, acknowledge it. Don't ever fall into the trap of thinking, "Larry knows how much I loved the new pen!" or "I said thank you on the way into the office—that's enough." If you want your thank-you to count, it has to be written down. It's the best way to solidify business relationships and pave the way for future favors.

Writing isn't just thinking

Writing is a complex physiological activity. It involves your muscles. It involves vision. It involves a kind of inner voice, one that "says" the words as they're written. It involves a kind of inner ear, one that "hears" the words as they're written.

Briefings

247

E-mail English

E-mail English is probably a little different from the English you've studied in school and read in the press. Because e-mail has to get its message across right away, some of the trappings of literary English fall by the wayside. E-mail English is closer to speech than it is to the newspaper or textbook. It takes cues from how we talk, preferring one-word sentences and a conversational tone to complex sentences and lofty vocabulary. Here are some features to keep in mind:

—Announce the main point of the e-mail in the first sentence whenever possible.

—Keep paragraphs short.

—Use plenty of white space between paragraphs to help the reader navigate the e-mail.

—Furnish headers to encourage skimming.

—Follow most-important-to-least-important, or general-to-specific paragraph structure.

—Keep sentences short.

—Use one-word sentences.

—Favor a subject-verb-complement sentence structure.

—Don't censure the "I" pronoun.

—Prefer direct, clear vocabulary.

—Opt for contractions.

—Feel comfortable employing the dash (—).

—Use technical language and jargon wisely.

—Be wary of SMS abbreviations in a business context.

—Shun decorative layout and inappropriate visual effects.

—Remember that your e-mail has unseen readers.

Sentence Patterns

Grammarians argue about what, exactly, is a sentence. Usually it has to have a subject and a verb. But e-mail has altered our view of the sentence, admitting nontraditional sentences into the fold. What's happened, in fact, is a shift from written sentence patterns to spoken sentence patterns. If your sentence can be spoken correctly, it can probably be written correctly in E-mail English, too.

Entry-level sentences

These are the sentences patterns you need in order to be a player.

One-Word Sentences:

—*Yes!*

—*Wrong.*

—*OK?*

Nontraditional Sentences:

—*Just as I thought.*

—*After a bit.*

—*So what.*

Simple Subject/Verb:

—*Jeremy waited.*

—*Rachel refused.*

Subject/Verb/Complement:

—*Raja looked at the map.*

—*He held the pointer.*

Compound Subject/Verb/Compliment:

—*The Chief Information Officer and Chief Executive met with the press.*

—*Design, manufacture, and distribution are the firm's strong points.*

Subject/Compound Verb/Complement:

—*The prospect listened and asked questions.*

—*The sales rep organized, reviewed, and prepared his speech.*

Sentence/FANBOYS Conjunction/Sentence:

(FANBOYS conjunctions are: For, And, Nor, But, Or, Yet, So. They are preceded by a comma.)

—*The team was thrilled with the news, so they all had lunch together.*

—*The market rebounded, but the gains were short-lived.*

Introductory Clause/Base Sentence:

(Introductory clauses begin with linking words such as "after," "when" and "because." Or they begin with an "ing" verb such as "thinking." When an introductory clause heads a sentence, it is usually followed by a comma.)

—*Since the margins were good, Tusin decided to sell.*

—*Noting the audience's curiosity, the speaker explained his proposal.*

Base Sentence/Terminal Clause:

—*She was for the new procedure if it eased congestion at the posts.*

—*The employee seemed shy because it was his first job.*

Ladder-climbing sentences

These sentence patterns build on the previous basic formulae. Because short, crisp sentences are preferred in e-mail, you don't want to rely on long, complex sentence structures—particularly if you're uncertain as to how a sentence is put together! *When in doubt, keep it short.* But if you're ready, occasionally using these and other complex sentences in your e-mails demonstrates confidence, knowledge, and flair.

Subject/Nonessential Modifier/Verb/Complement:

(A nonessential modifier is one that can be removed from the sentence without harming its structure or meaning. A nonessential modifier is surrounded by commas.)

—*The graphics, complete with 3D modules, were impressive.*

—*The manager, who had worked in development before, was an easy fit.*

Subject/Essential Modifier/Verb Complement:

(An Essential Modifier can't be removed from the sentence without changing its meaning.)

—*The product that won the reliability award was new to the market.*

—*The decision that was taken this morning marks a strategic change.*

Sentence/Adverbial Conjunction/Sentence:

(Adverbial conjunctions include accordingly, also, besides, consequently, conversely, furthermore, hence, however, in fact, in short, indeed, instead, likewise, meanwhile, moreover, namely, nevertheless, nonetheless, notwithstanding, otherwise, rather, still, then, therefore, and thus. They are preceded by a semicolon and followed by a comma.)

—*The market braced for the assault; accordingly, the index plunged.*

—*Publicity is necessary; otherwise, the consumer is left out of the loop.*

Subject/Verb Clause/Verb Claude/and Verb Clause:

(Because each verb comes with its own compliment, this sentence patterns allows you to pack in a lot of information in a single sentence unit.)

—*The new security procedures require full employee compliance, necessitate a thorough review of breach history, and promise a significant, if not total, reduction in press leaks.*

—*The Web-direct invoices facilitate payment fees and schedules, significantly reduce labor costs, streamline accounting, and promise shorter turn-around.*

Introductory Clause/Introductory Clause/(and)
Introductory Clause/Verb/Complement:

(This sentence pattern suggests how repetition can be used to structure a longer sentence unit.)

—*If you like to work hard, if you enjoy a challenge, if you consider yourself a "people person," then you'll want to be a part of our team.*

—*Because the job is unusually complex, because it involves lots of overtime and significant travel, and because it will be at least six months before you see results, you should think twice before signing the contract.*

Punctuation

Oh dear! The comma! One grammar book lists 47 uses for the comma, followed by rule 48, "Don't overuse the comma." How, one wonders, could a writer *not* overuse the comma when there are 47 rules for usage? And what about differences of opinion with regard to those rules? Some newspapers, for example, prefer a serial comma, as in, "I bought bread, milk, and cheese," while others eschew the comma before the "and."

But not all rules of punctuation are subject to interpretation, thank heavens. And e-mail writers don't have to know every teeny tiny point about punctuation to write effective, coherent e-mails. They just have to know the main rules for the sentence patterns most likely to crop up in an e-mail context. And they have to be consistent in following those rules.

The good news is that most writers have already assimilated the major do's and don'ts of punctuation—it's the difference between a hyphen (-) and dash (—) that brings them down. But with a couple minutes of review, and an effort to commit guidelines to memory, the sticky points can be eradicated. Forever.

Entry-Level punctuation

These are the ones you *must* have in order to write effective e-mails:

Period:

—Use it to mark the end of a sentence or abbreviations.

   Nontraditional Sentence: *Nope.*

   Traditional Sentence: *She signed the contract.*

   Abbreviations: *He was earning his Ph.D.*

Question Mark:

—Use it to mark a direct question.

   After a word: *Why?*

   After a sentence: *Are you ready to sign?*

Exclamation Mark:

—Use it to show emotion.

After a word: *Thanks!*

After a sentence: *Your thoughtfulness is appreciated!*

Comma:

—Use it to mark pauses between parts of a sentence.

Date: *On Saturday, July 22, 2006, he signed the check.*

After an introductory clause: *Because of the transportation strike, the meeting was postponed.*

Before a FANBOYS conjunction (For, And, Nor, Boy, Or, Yet, So): *The figures were encouraging, but management remained cautious.*

In a simple series: *The news was surprising, welcome, and leveled the playing field.*

Dash:

—Use it to join parts of a sentence.

Before a terminal clause: *The marketing campaign was an overall success better than we thought.*

Between two sentences: *The finances department complained about the new policies—it did nothing to change them.*

Colon:

—Use it to append information.

After an emphatic initial word: *Look: I'm ready when you are.*

Before a list: *She thought the problem could be fixed, provided: supplies keep pace with production; distribution maintains quality controls and on-time delivery; and publicity blankets the customer base.*

Semicolon:

—Use it to join closely linked components.

In a complex series: *The property had a swimming pool with an open waterfall; two tennis courts, one with a clay surface and one with grass; gardens with native flowers, bushes and shrubs; and a terrace area with fountains, shade trees, hammocks, and potted plants.*

Quotation Marks:

—Use them to mark a direct quotation from speech or a document.

Direct quotes from speech: *Her comment was, "You're the specialist, not me."*

Direct quotes from documents: *The letter states, "The patent is exempted from tertiary claims stemming from residual rights."*

Ladder-climbing marks of punctuation

Once you've mastered the basic usages of punctuation, it's time to strut your stuff. Proper usage of the following marks will score points with higher-ups and earn respect from colleagues and reports.

Comma:

—Use it to mark pauses between parts of a sentence.

Before and after an internal modifier: *Ms. Rosselli, who was new to the team, suggested a change in communication strategy.*

Before a terminal modifier: *I was pleased with the results, given how hard and how long we'd worked.*

In a complex series: *The new offices featured solar-generated power sources, full-spectrum lighting, wood and cork furniture, and rattan carpets.*

Hyphen:

—Use it to join words.

Closely linked adjectives: *The new employee wrote science-fiction stories for the company site.*

Closely linked nouns: *The break-in was widely publicized.*

Closely linked verbs: *He was a fill-in for her last Saturday.*

Dash:

—Use it to join parts of a sentence.

Before a terminal word: *Cummings was right—again.*

Around an emphatic modifier: *The HR Manager agreed—reluctantly—to the new hire.*

Colon:

—Use it to append information.

Before an emphatic terminal word: *The supervisor understood what the problem was: money.*

Semicolon:

—Use it to join closely linked components.

Between linked sentences: *The response was enthusiastic; profits soared.*

Between two sentences united by adverbial conjunctions: *Katen made the decision; consequently, the managers were pleased.*

Parentheses:

—Use them to append incidental information.

The receptionist took the guest to the office (the security escort was absent).

The meal was impressive. (But too costly!)

Ellipsis:

—Use it to show that information has been purposefully omitted (*three* dots if the ellipsis is inside a sentence, *four* dots if it's at the end).

In a quote: *He said, "The deal was worth our serious attention in...M&A, but that the company needed to restructure."*

At the end of a sentence: *I told him that Arthur's idea was a problematic one....*

Quotation Marks:

—Use them to mark words used in unusual ways.

Special usage: *The team leader said the prototype was "almost" completed.*

Emphasis

No doubt about it: Some ideas are more important than others. Knowing how to draw attention to the main ideas and slot the supporting information in the right place are essential e-mail skills. Luckily, there are many ways of emphasizing in English. Sometimes the techniques work well together...and sometimes they don't. Like too much sugar in the iced tea, too much emphasis can deflect the reader's attention, particularly in the business world where restraint receives high marks and effusiveness is often perceived as defensive. Use your emphasis wisely, and remember...a little bit goes a long way.

Layout:

—The first sentence in an e-mail is the most emphatic because that's where the reader decides to read on...or not.

—The first sentences of paragraphs are automatically emphasized, because they announce what the paragraph is about. They're prime bait for readers who skim.

—Words or sentences surrounded by white space also receive extra attention because the skimmer can latch on to them quickly.

Paragraph Order:

—First and last paragraphs receive more emphasis than middle paragraphs, in the sense that readers are more apt to skim—or even read—the beginning and end of a document than they are its middle.

Headers:

—Headers can steal emphasis from paragraphs to the point that some readers only read the headers and skip the paragraphs.

Capitals:

—A word or sentence in capitals gets the reader's attention, but too many capitals start to shout. A slew of capitals alienates the reader, because no one likes to be yelled at.

Italics/Underlining:

—Italicized/underlined words and sentences are the traditional way of obtaining stylistic emphasis in a text. Italics/underlining have yielded to capitals in informal e-mail, but maintain their prestige in more formal or official documents.

Bold:

—Bold is best used to contrast with other forms of stylistic emphasis in an e-mail, such as italics/underlining and capitals. Some writers, however, use bold face type for primary stylistic emphasis, forgoing capitals and italics.

Indentation:

—You can draw attention to details by indenting them. The more indented the text is, the more detailed or specific its information.

Repetition:

—Conscious word repetition is an easy way to create emphasis. Starting three or four sentences with "Our company..." as the subject draws attention to...the company! The key to using word repetition is to couple it with parallel grammatical structure so that the repeated words appear in a similar grammatical context.

Metaphors and Images:

—Slowing a text down by furnishing a metaphor or an image creates emphasis through analogy. If we say that writing effective e-mail is a little like learning how to ride a bike—once you learn how to do it, you always know how to do it—we've drawn attention to the fact that writing skill is something you can't lose.

Specificity:

—Specificity creates emphasis by sustaining the reader's attention. If an e-mail argues for a pay raise by detailing a list of accomplishments, the point that a raise is due becomes emphatic.

Word Choice:

—Rare, literary words—though usually frowned on in E-mail English— can create emphasis on special occasions. If I say that a coworker's behavior was "inappropriate," I've used a neutral, business-as-usual term for unacceptable behavior. But if I say a person's behavior was "reprehensible," I've emphasized just how bad it was.

Color:

—Black typeface rules in business, because it sends a no-nonsense, authoritative message. It's also easier on the eyes. Confine colored type and backgrounds to special occasions, but be wary of color in your normal e-mail. You don't want to appear frivolous or juvenile.

Multiple Emphasis:

—Complex e-mails, long e-mails, and attachments sometimes call for different kinds of emphasis. In this case, business writers assign different meanings to different stylistic effects. They might use bold for main points, capitals for not-to-be-missed details, and italics for special insights. The idea here is to figure out a pattern for emphasis and stick with it. The different kinds of emphasis modulate the reader's attention and allow him or her to self-navigate the text.

De-Emphasizing:

—The best way of de-emphasizing something in English is to bury it. If you put something disagreeable in a subordinate clause within a complex sentence and place that sentence in the middle of a longish paragraph in the middle of a document, it's as camouflaged as it can possibly be.

Rhetorical Modes

Writing strategies called "rhetorical modes" have their roots in the ancient art of declamation when rhetoricians could convince everyone within earshot to do what they wanted them to do. These rhetoricians used description, exposition, and cause and effect, just as we do today. Rhetorical modes are as likely to crop up in the boardroom as they are in an e-mail. The rhetorical modes have been hanging around for thousands of years because they *work*.

Rhetorical modes provide *strategies* for harassing information and presenting it to a reader in order to persuade him or her to act or think in a specific way. Rhetorical modes aren't static. They're not exact "maps" of document organization. They're more like motors. They provide energy. That's why they're called the "rhetorical modes," with emphasis on "mode." They move information from the speaker to the hearer, or from the writer to the reader.

An e-mail, for example, that defines what is meant by "competence" uses the "definition" mode, with each paragraph devoted to discussing a different aspect of what is meant by the term "competence." One paragraph, for instance, might address "technical" competence, while another might address "ethical" competence, and so on. Or consider an e-mail arguing for a promotion that uses paragraphs of narration (relating the employee's accomplishments over the past two years), description (describing the employee's character), and exposition (explaining why the promotion should be granted now). Within the paragraph of exposition, in turn, there might be a sentence using exemplification. And the sentence using exemplification might contain a clause of description.

Because these strategies shuffle, blend, and combine, they might seem a bit confusing at first, but in fact, we use them all the time in English-language conversation. The challenge comes in recognizing that we've engaged a particular rhetorical mode in a piece of writing. When we're conscious of which mode we're using, we have a better chance of making it work to our advantage.

The more you master e-mail English, the more useful knowledge of the rhetorical modes becomes.

Description: describes persons, places, and abstract things

Spatial 1: moves from panorama to specific detail or vise versa

An e-mail describing the new company headquarters, beginning with the layout of the site and ending with the logo above the front door.

Spatial 2: moves clockwise or counterclockwise

An e-mail describing a new Webpage, beginning with the top banner and moving to the left, center, right.

Spatial 3: moves from top to bottom or vice versa

An e-mail describing a new org chart, beginning at the bottom and moving toward the top.

Abstract 1: moves from a general quality to a specific quality, or vice versa

An e-mail describing a new software product, beginning with the concept of intuition and ending on the number for voice support.

Abstract 2: moves from the most important point to the least important point

An e-mail summarizing a conference call that begins with the outcome of the meeting and ends by describing a minor point for follow-up.

Narration: narrates information in sequential order

Chronology: foregrounds temporal markers in the event *sequence* (time, day, year), ordinals (first, second, third), or linking words (then, next, finally)

An e-mail narrating the play-by-play of a conference call.

Process: uses steps in a sequence to emphasize a specific *result*

An e-mail narrating the firm's procedure for reimbursement of company expenses, from application on the intranet to bank receipts.

Cause-and-Effect: emphasizes the consequential *link* between the steps in a sequence

An e-mail narrating a climb up the career ladder, from entry level to the boardroom.

Comparison and Contrast (CC): compares the similarities between two or more things and contrasts their differences

Weighted CC: Object A receives more discussion than Object B.

An e-mail with three paragraphs devoted to the palette on Macintosh computers and one paragraph devoted to the palette on standard PCs.

Equal CC: Object A and Object B discussed in terms of the same points and receiving about the same number of words each.

An e-mail with paragraphs devoted to the price, co-pay, and coverage of one dental plan followed by paragraphs devoted to the price, co-pay, and coverage of another dental plan.

Exemplification: exemplifies an idea through illustration

Brief Exemplification: uses one or more brief examples or illustrations, often with one clause or sentence per example.

An e-mail communicating a new return policy, with several one-sentence examples of improper returns.

Extended Exemplification: uses one long example discussed over several paragraphs.

An e-mail introducing a new superconductor, with three paragraphs exemplifying the product's performance in +30 C conditions.

Definition: defines a term, concept, or series of ideas

Brief Definition: uses one or more brief examples to communicate how particular terms are being used in a document, often with one sentence per definition.

An e-mail discussing the company's harassment policy, with the terms "inappropriate remarks," "inappropriate e-mails" and "inappropriate touching" each defined in a separate sentence

Extended Definition: concentrates on defining a specific term in one or more paragraphs

An e-mail defining what is meant by the legal concept of "residual rights," with the breadth of the definition in one paragraph, the limitations of the definition in another paragraph, mitigating circumstances in the next, and so on.

Exposition: explains action, behavior or events by highlighting facts and reasons so that a reader understands "why" and/or "how" the action, behavior, or event occurred

Simple Exposition: explicates the phenomenon in a sentence or two

An e-mail asking Human Resources to hire a new financial analyst that explains in one sentence that the current analyst resigned.

Complex Exposition: combines various rhetorical modes in order to explain the phenomenon in depth

An e-mail highlighting how and why a particular product had marketplace success, with one paragraph summarizing the competition at the moment of entry, another summarizing product differentiation, the next describing brand loyalty, and so on.

Argument: persuades the reader to change his or her mind or to take a particular course of action

Reader-Based Arguments: appeal to the reader's self-interest

An e-mail announcing a telephone plan that will save the reader money.

Emotional Arguments: engage the reader's emotions in order to persuade

An e-mail soliciting donations for a Children's Hospital Fund.

Authority Arguments: coming from and/or invoking one or more authorities respected by the reader

An e-mail announcing that the team will have to redo a report based on the observations of upper management.

Objective Arguments: persuade the reader though impersonal facts and reasons

An e-mail explaining the closure of the company that uses figures and statistics to make a clear case for insolvency.

Complex Arguments: combine various rhetorical modes to persuade through emotion, facts, authorities, and self-interest

An e-mail arguing for company expansion that begins by appealing to the reader's emotions by discussing company pride, then invokes authority of the company president, refers to figures to substantiate opinions, and finally describes how the readers will benefit from the change.

Editing and Proofing Strategies

Correcting an e-mail is relatively easy…once you recognize where the errors are! The hardest part is spotting the portions of a document that need work, refinement, and/or a little extra attention. That's why professional editors on the Web, in the press, and in publishing work in teams: If one pair of eyes doesn't see the error, then usually another pair of eyes will.

The business world is lonely in this regard, because we often have to edit and proofread our own documents. Deadlines can turn on the pressure, while the stress of multitasking may render us inattentive just at the moment when we should be concentrating. The result is that we don't see the errors in our e-mails until later—when we're looking over what we sent. And then it's too late. The trick is learning to see the errors and correct them *before* we push the send button. Here are some tips that should help:

—Change type size. Sometimes just stepping up the size of the type allows you to visualize the errors.

—Change type font. Turning an e-mail written in Helvetica into one written in Courier does more than alter the e-mail's appearance—it also allows you to see it afresh.

—Take a break and come back to it. Even a short break—walking to the coffee machine and back—can make a difference.

—Print it out if time allows. Looking at a piece of paper is different than looking at a screen. Errors tend to pop out when they're printed.

—Read it in a loud voice. A loud and forceful voiced reading of a text can force errors out of hiding.

—Read it backwards. Begin with the last sentence and work your way backwards through the document, sentence by sentence. This technique neutralizes narrative momentum and allows you to see each sentence as a unit.

Keep correcting until you can't find any more errors. You can't see *all* the errors *at once*—you only pick up on a couple at a time. All the more reason to keep at it until the document turns up clean…at least twice.

Bibliography

Alfred, G. J., C.T. Brusaw, and Walter E. Oliu. *The Business Writer's Handbook*. 7th ed. Boston: Bedford/St. Martin's, 2003.

Anson, C. M., and Robert A. Schwegler. *The Longman Handbook for Writers and Readers*. 2nd ed. New York, NY: Addison-Wesley Educational Publishers Inc., 2000.

Azar, Betty Schrampfer. *Understanding and Using English Grammar*. Englewood Cliffs: Prentice-Hall, Inc., 1989.

Behrens, L., and Leonard J. Rosen. *The Allyn & Bacon Handbook*. 4th ed. Needham Heights: Allyn & Bacon, 2000.

Bell, Arthur H. *Business Communication: Toward 2000*. Cincinnati: South-Western Publishing Co., 1992.

Bender, James F. *Make Your Business Letters Make Friends*. New York: McGraw-Hill Book Company, Inc., 1952.

Bly, Robert. *Webster's New World Letter Writing Handbook*. Indianapolis: Wiley Publishing, 2004.

Boros, Claudine L. *The Essentials of Business Writing*. Piscataway: Research and Education Association, 1996.

Brittney, Lynn. *e-mail@nd business letter writing*. London: Foulsham, 2000.

Broukal, Milada. *In-A-Flash: Grammar for the TOEFL*. 4th ed. Lawrenceville: Peterson's, 2002.

Claire, Elizabeth. *Dangerous English 2000!* 3rd ed. McHenry: Delta Publishing Company, 1998.

Cross, Wilbur. *Small Business Model Letter Book*. Englewood Cliffs: Prentice Hall, 1992.

DeVries, Mary A. *Internationally Yours: Writing and Communicating Successfully in Today's Global Marketplace*. Boston: Houghton Mifflin Company, 1994.

————. *The New American Handbook of Letter Writing*. Avenel, NJ: 1993.

Dodds, Jack. *The Ready Reference Handbook*. Needham Heights: Allyn & Bacon, 1997.

Flynn, Nancy and Tom Flynn. *Writing Effective E-Mail*. Boston, MA: Fifty-Minute Series Book, 2003.

Fulwiler, T., and Alan R. Hayakawa. *The Blair Handbook*. Upper Saddle River: Pearson Education, Inc., 2003.

Garner, Bryan A. *Legal Writing in Plain English*. Chicago: University of Chicago Press, 2001.

Gifis, Steven H. *Dictionary of Legal Terms: A Simplified Guide to the Language of Law*. 3rd ed. Hauppauge: Barron's Educational Series, Inc., 1998

Hacker, Diana. *Rules for Writers*. Boston: Bedford, 2000.

Hodges, J. C., and Mary E. Whitten. *Harbrace College Handbook*. 10th ed. New York: Harcourt Brace Jovanovich, Inc., 1986.

Hughes, E., J. Silverman, and Diana Roberts Wienbroer. *Rules of Thumb for Business Writers*. New York: McGraw-Hill, 2002.

Layton, Marcia. *The Complete Idiot's Guide to Terrific Business Writing*. New York: Alpha Books, 1996.

Lindsell-Roberts, Sheryl. *Business Letter Writing*. New York: Macmillan General Reference, 1995.

Locker, Kitty O. *Business and Administrative Communication*. 3rd ed. Boston: Richard D. Irwin, Inc., 1995.

Lunsford, A., and Cheryl Glenn. *The New St. Martin's Handbook*. Boston: Bedford/St. Martin's, 1999.

Markel, Mike. *Technical Communication*. 6th ed. Boston: Bedford/St. Martin's, 2001.

Merriam-Webster, ed. *Merriam-Webster's Guide to Business Correspondence, Second Edition*. Springfield: Meriam-Webster, Inc., 2002.

Muckian, Michael and John Woods. *The Business Letter Handbook*. Avon: Adams Media Corporation, 1996.

Neal, Dorothy. *Effective Letters for Business, Professional and Personal Use*. Perrysburg: Neal Publications, Inc., 2000.

Piotrowski, Maryann V. *Effective Business Writing*. New York: HarperCollins Publishers, Inc., 1996.

Rozakis, Laurie. *The Literate Executive*. New York: McGraw-Hill, 2000.

Sabin, William A. *The Gregg Reference Manual*. 9th ed. New York: Glencoe/McGraw-Hill, 2001.

Troyka, Lynn Quitman. *Simon & Schuster Handbook for Writers*. 4th ed. Upper Saddle River: Prentice Hall, 1996.

Volokh, Eugene. *Academic Legal Writing: Law Review Articles, Student Notes, and Seminar Papers*. New York: Foundation Press, 2003.

Index

About the Author

Dawn-Michelle Baude is an active corporate speaker specialized in global communications. She has lectured throughout Europe and Asia to businesses and alumni groups alike. An accomplished writing professional, she has written copy for Gucci perfumes, feature articles for *Reader's Digest* and *Vogue*, and co-authored a self-help best-seller, *Savoir Dire Non* (Flammarion, 2006), in addition to publishing widely in art criticism and poetry. In 2000, she began working as a writing consultant for IBM Corp. She holds an MA, an MFA, a DEA, and a Ph.D. in English. A 2005-06 Senior Fulbright Scholar in Creative Writing, she teaches at the American University of Paris.